CISO Wisdom - Paperback

Cybersecurity Untangled
Sammy Basu

Copyright © [2024] by [Sammy Basu]

All rights reserved. No portion of this book may be reproduced in any form without written permission from the publisher or author, except as permitted by U.S. copyright law.

Contents

Dedication	1
Introduction	2
The Problem	4
Lords of the Underworld	13
The Price of a Password	25
Distributed Data	43
Security Skills Shortage	61
The Art of Simplicity	80
Defense in Depth	98
Protectors of the Castle	119
Social Engineering	150
The Boy who cried Wolf	161
The Impact of AI	173
Ransomware Attacks	183
Risky Business	194

The Hammer of Compliance	209
The New Sheriff in Town	218
The 90-Day Playbook	230
Acknowledgements	240
About the Author	241

Dedication

This book is dedicated to humanistic philosopher and educator Daisaku Ikeda (1928–2023). He dedicated his life to fostering a lasting culture of peace through dialogue. His writings on the theme of never giving up, choosing hope and courage has been a source of encouragement for countless people across the globe. Corporate cybersecurity is rewarding, stressful and often a thankless job. Ikeda believed that open dialogue is the key to solving the problems facing us today. He said "The courage to meet and talk with people is absolutely crucial. Choosing dialogue is itself the triumph of peace and of humanity." Based on his philosophy, lets break down the silos of corporate cybersecurity and have a dialogue with each other around how we can solve this problem that's plaguing all our lives today.

Introduction

We have approached this book with a focus on industry data, solutions, and resources. It serves as a guidebook for us in how we deliver service to our clients. We hope that you, the reader, can gain some wisdom from our experiences in cybersecurity. Initially, we started writing this with the bitterness and complaints about things not working. However, we realized that this approach is not helpful.

This book can also be a sounding board for professionals struggling to make a difference in a challenging corporate environment. If you are a business owner, you can review your business risks from the summaries and recurring patterns we captured from various data breach reports. If you're not in the field of cybersecurity but are curious about its concepts, you can read quotes and analogies that compare it to daily life.

The opinions expressed are subjective and any resemblance to real-life entities is purely coincidental. The word 'cybersecurity' can be a mouthful, so we have occasionally referred to it as 'security'. If you are a security professional, you can look at the tools and resources available to mitigate these gaps. The list is not comprehensive. Its more of a start and we welcome your feedback on what else you'd like to see there.

We hope there is something in this book for everyone. We've worked on this book along with daily job and commitments. The hardest part was wrapping it up in the unfinished form that it is in. So here it is, our six months of research into the complex world of cybersecurity. This is our first book. Please be gentle with us. Thank you.

Chapter 1: The Problem

A view from the escalator

"There are two types of companies: those that have been hacked, and those who don't yet know they have been hacked."
-Former Cisco CEO, John Chambers

I had never been to a RSA Conference before. Having heard about it from colleagues and clients I had always wanted to go to one but never made it because of work, family, or other priorities. Bitten by the bug to write a book on cybersecurity and enticed by the thought of collecting cool vendor swag, t-shirts, caps et al I made the long drive from Los Angeles to San Francisco to clear my head and get inspired. The enormity of the space, swarming with vendor booths and industry leaders was awe-inspiring. Energized by the passion, the discussions, and the presentations I promised to myself to come back again next year. However, skepticism crept in on the way back as we crawled through San Francisco traffic. Despite all of these shows, conferences, and brilliance we still haven't been able to solve the cybersecurity conundrum as attacks continue unabated. Are we on the right track to solve the problem or are we just beating around the bush learning through trial and error?

According to the predictions from Statista Market Insights[1] the cost of cybercrime will continue to skyrocket for the next 5 years. The Global Risks Report by the World Economic Forum places cyberattacks as one of the top global risks that can affect business operations, financial stability, and geopolitical landscapes. Anyone who follows cybersecurity news knows that cyberattacks are getting out of control. From casinos to children's hospitals, nothing is spared, nothing is out of bounds. Nation states are launching cyberattacks on critical infrastructure, nuclear facilities, and space stations. Scammers are depleting senior citizens of their life savings. Our personal information, social security numbers, and dates of birth are traded on the dark web. Ransomware attacks are the new normal.

---

1. https://www.statista.com/

Medical institutions are being forced to suspend operations, patient care and prescriptions.

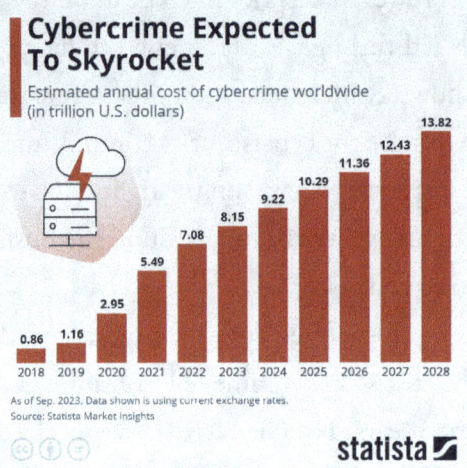

Somebody please help!

In the United States alone, there are 1.2 million cybersecurity professionals. 4000+ cybersecurity vendors and 10000+ products[2]. All of them come with the promise of a panacea. And yet the global annual cost of global cybercrime continues to rise. How did we get here? Are there any solutions in sight? The insiders in corporate circles are starting to lose hope. "It doesn't matter what we do, we'll still get hacked." Well, the same applies to many other things in life for e.g. driving under incremental conditions. No matter how skilled you are, there's a chance of getting

---

2. https://dashboard.it-harvest.com/dashboard

into an collision in the road. But that doesn't stop us from driving, we still need to go to places. Fearing cyberattacks shouldn't prevent us from enjoying the convenience of the online world.

Priorities, Priorities

Business owners consider cybersecurity a cost center instead of a business enabler as they remain focused on growth of the company. Security professional blame employees for security lapses that introduced malware into the organization. Technology leaders only invest in technical based solutions even though studies have shown that 4 out 5 security incidents were started by human error, negligence or lack of awareness. Compliance programs are great in introducing a baseline of security practices however they may end up overlooking the unknown factors that cause security breaches.

Different perspectives

The urgency and attitude to cybersecurity varies with the culture of the organization. It's a gatekeeper in Government institutions, fear factor at financial establishments, background actor in the entertainment industry, risk averse in the insurance sector and a risk taker at startups that dares to cut corners with the thrill of innovation.

The attackers are aware of these and change their modus operandi based on the industry they're targeting.

Its not you, its me

Small and medium-sized businesses(SMBs) are targeted more frequently because they lack dedicated security resources to detect and defend against such attacks. When we speak with SMB owners about investing in security initiatives they are genuinely perplexed. Why on earth would someone attack me they ask? I am a good person. We're a small business. Why? Cyber criminals may borrow George Constanza's breakup quote on Seinfeld "It's not you, it's me." "There's nothing personal about it, we're stealing your data to make money. It's not you, it's me.

Breaches and Root Causes

According to Verizon's Data Breach Report, the modus operandi behind a data breach is not a zero-day exploit or a carefully constructed highly sophisticated attack. It usually starts with one of these three security lapses : misuse of login credentials, phishing attacks, and exploitation of unpatched vulnerabilities. We analyzed some recent profile breaches and their root causes. Here they are.

United HealthCare Breach : 2024

During the United HealthCare group breach of February 2024 almost every hospital in the country was hampered in their operations. United Healthcare attributed the breach to failures in supply chain security. Hackers breached the computer system of a UnitedHealth Group subsidiary and released ransomware after breaching the password on a portal that didn't have multi-factor authentication enabled. The cyberattack shut down operations at hospitals and pharmacies for more than a week. The ransomware gang that caused this attack claimed to have stolen over six terabytes of data, including sensitive medical records. Third parties in the supply chain run a higher risk because they may not have the resources to prevent a breach. The cyberattack on United Healthcare has surpassed $2.3 billion. Root Cause : Legacy server that didn't have Multi-factor authentication enabled.

Microsoft Email Breach : 2024

Microsoft's corporate email accounts were breached, and sensitive emails and communications disclosed. The attackers used a brute-force technique where common passwords are 'sprayed' against multiple accounts. The attackers got into an old test account that didn't have multi-factor authentication and used it to move laterally within Microsoft's network. Root Cause: Legacy account without Multi-factor Authentication.

MGM Resorts Cyberattack : 2023

The perpetrators used a social engineering attack tactic known as "Vishing" for voice impersonating an IT administrator locked out of the system and needed to restore access. The impersonation was life-like. Once the attackers gained privileged access, they exploited a security vulnerability in the identity management system. MGM had to suspend operations for six days, while the attacker's sensitive personal information including dates of birth, driver's license numbers and social security numbers. Root Cause: Social Engineering attack.

23andMe Data Breach : 2023

Hackers managed to sneak into a few user accounts because those accounts didn't have that extra layer of security – you know, multi-factor authentication (MFA). Once they were in, they went on a data-grabbing spree, scooping up info from other users who had signed up for this "DNA Relatives" feature just a week earlier. It's a classic case of how a seemingly small security lapse – skipping MFA – can have a domino effect, leading to a much bigger breach. It's like leaving the front door unlocked; once someone's inside, they can access a lot more than just the entryway.

Colonial Pipeline Ransomware Attack : 2021

Colonial Pipeline suffered a crippling ransomware attack in May 2021, causing serious disruptions. A compromised password of a VPN account for a former employee allowed hackers to steal 100GB of data and encrypt IT systems. The attack led to fuel shortages, panic-buying, and a spike in gas prices, prompting a state of an emergency declaration by President Biden. Colonial Pipeline paid a 75-bitcoin ransom, and operations resumed after six days. Root cause: Disclosed credentials for VPN account without multi-factor authentication.

SolarWinds Supply Chain Attack : 2020

The attackers exploited insecure coding practices to insert malicious code and launch a supply chain cyberattack on SolarWinds customers which included large government institutions. Root cause: Insecure software development practices.

Capital One Data Breach : 2019

The bad actor was able to access more than 100 million Capital One customers' accounts and credit card applications by exploiting insecurely configured web application firewalls in cloud-hosted infrastructure. Root Cause: Security misconfiguration of hosting infrastructure

Equifax Data Breach : 2017

The attackers gained access to the network by exploiting an unpatched security vulnerability in a public facing web server. The data breach exposed the personal information of 147 million people. Root Cause: Failure to patch a known software vulnerability in a timely manner.

Chapter 2: Lords of the Underworld

The Wild Wild West

"If you know the enemy and know yourself, you need not fear the result of a hundred battles. If you know yourself but not the enemy, for every victory gained you will also suffer a defeat. If you know neither the enemy nor yourself, you will succumb in every battle."
                    -Sun Tzu, The Art of War

The Wild West of the Dark Web

Imagine a country with no rules. There's no centralized government, it's a place of chaos and anarchy ruled by lawlessness and anonymity. A digital country like that exists today and it's called the Dark Web! The Dark Web is the underbelly of the internet. Nobody knows your true identity, your presence is anonymized through an underground interconnected network of devices also known as the onion. You cannot go to the dark web without using a specialized browser called tor. In the dark web our darkest instincts come into play. Cybercriminals use it for weapons, drugs, selling and buying people's personal and banking information, corporate data, passwords and security exploits. You can find hackers for hire. Some of them are highly intelligent, but struggle with social interaction or grapple with mental health challenges. Some are running underground criminal business syndicates. Many lack formal schooling in cybersecurity, instead honing their skills through online forums and self-learning. They joined hacking forums and learned how to break into other people's computers. Entering the forum is not a straightforward process. Someone has to vouch for you. You need to verify your identity or buy a paid membership. The more notorious forums have as many as 400,000 active users. They sell the latest hacking tools, exploitation toolkits, phishing emails, voice impersonators, and information on corporate and government security vulnerabilities.[1]

Some younger cybercriminals are not mature enough to distinguish right from wrong or comprehend the moral implications of their actions. Daniel Kelley is a reformed black hat hacker. Kelley was 18 years old when he got arrested and sentenced to four years in prison. Before his arrest, Kelley had little concept of the real-life world. He lived online for 18 hours a day and rarely left home. He was hacking websites, stealing data, and demanding ransom payments from business owners. Kelley was a lone wolf operator. He had Asperger's Syndrome, a developmental disorder found in high-functioning individuals who have an all-absorbing interest in specific topics and a hard time relating to others in social interactions. He's turned his life around and now focuses on security research and content writing.[2]

Ransomware gangs use the dark web to buy passwords and information of victim organizations from Initial Ac-

---

1. Europol(2024), Internet Organised Crime Threat Assessment (IOCTA)2024, Publications Office of the European Union, Luxembourg.

2. https://www.securityweek.com/hacker-conversations-inside-the-mind-of-daniel-kelley-ex-blackhat/

cess Brokers (IAB). IABs gain initial access into the victim's network and sell the secret information to other gangs. Each gang has their own specialized skill sets. One group specializes in developing malicious software code. The other group uses the code to hijack user privileges and launch crippling attacks. Another group manages the financial aspects of the business by negotiating and collecting the ransom payment.[3] IABs sell various types of access information such as privileged accounts, remote desktops, virtual private networks, web servers, access to remote monitoring tools, and active directories. To ensure credibility and seller reputation they provide evidence of verified access.

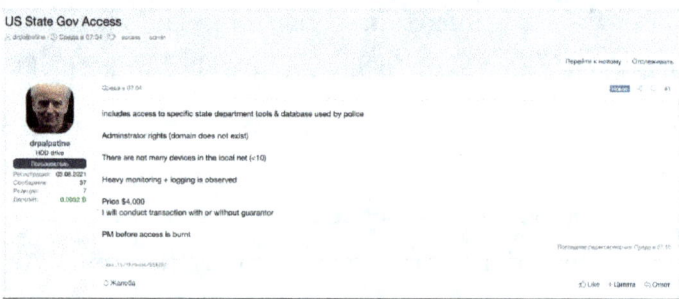

IABs selling information on the Dark Web

The market for this kind of access is growing fast. CrowdStrike research cited by Europol shows a 50% in-

---

3. https://ransomware.org/how-does-ransomware-work/active-defense-intrusion/credential-markets-and-initial-access-brokers/

crease in advertised access prices in 2024, reflecting rising demand from ransomware operators and other criminal buyers.

The Dark Web Marketplace

According to Europol's 2025 IOCTA report, personal data is now a core currency in the underground economy. Cybercriminals go after everything from login credentials to credit card numbers, medical records, and social media accounts. The Verizon 2025 Data Breach Investigations Report confirms the pattern: credential abuse, followed by vulnerability exploitation and phishing. The primary motivation remains financial gain. The lure of quick money cloaked with the anonymity of the dark web has turned intelligent individuals into cybercriminals. Nation-states are also using the dark web for espionage, to gather intelligence, disrupt adversaries, and gain a competitive edge. To steal intellectual property, internal government information, and military secrets. To adversely impact social and economic stability, national security, and diplomatic relations. There's also a group of solo operators driven by personal grievances, a thirst for power and revenge, or an intent to cause harm to others.

Tactics and Techniques

Victims are selected based on the type of tools available in the attacker's arsenal. For e.g. if the malware is tailored for manufacturing software then it is sprayed against the manufacturing infrastructure. If the malware is designed to steal credit card data, attackers target e-commerce sites that accept online payments. If the payment gateways contain a security vulnerability, then that vulnerability is used to compromise other sites that use the same payment gateway. When a software vulnerability was discovered within the MoveIT file transfer software the attackers targeted all organizations using this software, encrypted and exfiltrated their databases, and sold it on the Dark Web.

The adoption of new technologies and the complexity of our digital infrastructure have magnified the attack surface. But nothing has changed the economics of cybercrime faster than artificial intelligence. AI has reduced the time needed to craft a convincing phishing email. Attackers no longer need to be native English speakers or talented writers. Generative AI produces grammatically perfect, highly personalized messages at scale. IBM's 2025

Cost of a Data Breach Report found that 16% of breaches now involve attackers using AI, with AI-generated phishing accounting for 37% of those incidents and deepfake impersonation accounting for 35%. Europol's 2025 IOCTA report warns that large language models and generative AI are making social engineering tactics more convincing than ever.

The proliferation of AI tools on the dark web goes beyond phishing. Criminals use AI to generate fake IDs and online accounts, automate credential stuffing attacks that adapt in real time, create deepfake audio and video for voice impersonation scams, and repackage previously stolen data into fresh attack campaigns. The Identity Theft Resource Center identified a new trend in 2025 where hackers use AI to repackage old breach data to launch new waves of account takeover and fraud. Your stolen credentials from a 2019 breach get a second life.

Infostealers, a type of malware designed to extract personal data from infected devices, are thriving. One tool called Lumma infected over 394,000 Windows devices worldwide before being taken down by law enforcement in 2025. Along with phishing, there is vishing or voice impersonation, quishing or QR code impersonation, and smishing or SMS phishing. We are getting spam text messages with bad links almost every day. Attackers continue to target the human factor as our weakest line of defense, but now they have AI making every attack more convincing, more personalized, and harder to detect.

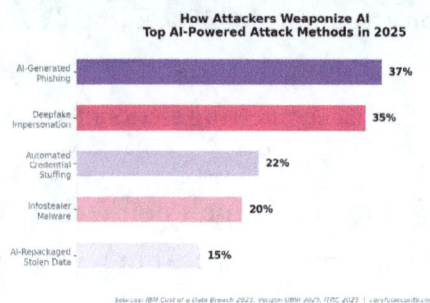

AI Pros and Cons

Criminal syndicates are peddling easy access to ransomware-as-a-service. Attackers are scanning the internet for vulnerabilities in publicly accessible systems. They purchase malware services that steal user login credentials from Web Browsers, FTP services, VPNs, and Email accounts. Then gain access through stolen credentials or exploiting vulnerabilities in the publicly accessible infrastructure. Penetration testing tools like Cobalt Strike and Metasploit are being used to gain a foothold and administrative password cracking tools like Mimikatz are used to gain access and escalate user privileges.

The economics of ransomware shifted in 2025. On-chain payment tracking by Chainalysis recorded roughly $820 million in ransomware payments. IBM's 2025 report found that 63% of ransomware victims declined to pay. But refusing to pay doesn't eliminate the cost. The average expense of an extortion or ransomware incident reached $5.08 million when disclosed by the attacker. And attackers have adapted. Instead of just encrypting data, many now skip the encryption entirely and simply steal the data, threatening to release it publicly. The ITRC's 2025 Annual Data Breach Report confirmed that ransomware incidents actually decreased, as attackers shifted to data theft and extortion without encryption. The business model evolved, but the threat didn't shrink. It just changed shape.

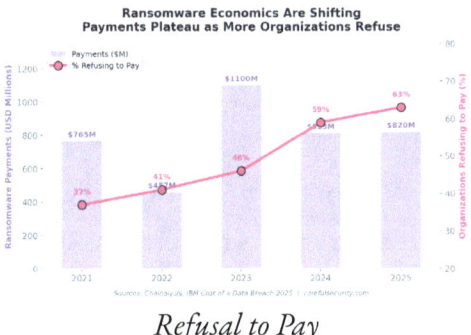

Refusal to Pay

Back in 2017, The Economist stated "The world's most valuable resource is no longer oil, but data." Today the dark web continues to facilitate trading of leaked databases, stolen credit cards, and corporate data for identity theft, financial fraud, and other nefarious activities. The price of credit card numbers is based on outstanding balance and spending limit. The price for login information to bank accounts is lower for Credit Union accounts and higher for Swiss bank accounts. Social Security numbers, dates of birth, our confidential health records: everything is up for sale.

Dark Web Price Menu 2025 Market Rates	
PERSONAL IDENTITY	
Social Security Number	6 – 15
Date of Birth + SSN + Address	15 – 65
Full Identity Package (Fullz)	30 – 100
Selfie Holding ID	100 – 120
FINANCIAL ACCESS	
Credit Card (with CVV)	17 – 120
Bank Login (Credit Union)	50 – 100
Bank Login (Major Bank)	100 – 500
Verified Crypto Account	400 – 1,170
DIGITAL ACCOUNTS	
Email Login (Gmail, Outlook)	5 – 15
Social Media Account	10 – 75
Streaming Service (Netflix, etc)	3 – 25
Corporate VPN/RDP Access	500 – 5,000+

Access with verified MFA bypass (stolen session cookies) commands a significant premium.
Sources: Privacy Affairs, TrustWave, SOCRadar (2023) | corelisecurity.com

Today's Menu

Dark web monitoring by Trustwave, SOCRadar, and Privacy Affairs shows prices remain consistent: basic PII like name and email sells for under $15 due to breach oversupply, while high-value access like verified bank logins and cryptocurrency accounts commands $1,000 or more. SSNs start at $6. Access with verified MFA bypass, such as stolen session cookies, commands a significant premium. The market runs like a legitimate business: Tor for anonymity, Monero for payment, escrow systems for trust.

Personally identifiable information or PII is any information record that can be used to identify an individual.

Examples include social security numbers, dates of birth, phone numbers, addresses, etc. The IBM 2025 Cost of a Data Breach Report captures the cost of a data breach based on the type of industry. Organizations with healthcare records make for the most lucrative targets due to the high market value of restricted healthcare information.

Any organization, regardless of size or perceived data value can be targeted by cyberattacks. Attackers are motivated by financial gain, disruption, or political and ideological reasons. All organizations must recognize their potential as targets and implement strong cybersecurity measures starting with attack surface management to monitor their security exposures.

MITRE ATT&CK Framework

The MITRE ATT&CK framework is like a detailed guidebook that explains all the different attack paths adversaries can use to break into our organizations. It demonstrates the different techniques adversaries may attempt to get a foothold, gain access, evade detection, and launch attacks. By studying the cyber-attack tactics we can implement stronger security measures to limit the damage and facilitate quick responses.

What This Means for Your Business

The dark web isn't an abstract concept from a movie. It's a functioning marketplace where your company's data has a price tag. Credit card numbers sell for $17 to $120. Bank account logins go for $100. A complete identity package costs about $1,000. Cybercriminals operate with the same business discipline as legitimate enterprises: specialized roles, subscription services, customer reviews, and escrow payments. Ransomware-as-a-service lets anyone with a credit card launch an attack. AI tools let anyone with a keyboard craft a convincing phishing email. The barrier to entry has never been lower. If your organization handles customer data, payment information, or health records, you are a target. Not because someone has a personal grudge. Because your data has a market value, and someone is willing to pay for it. The chapters that follow will show you how to make their job as difficult and expensive as possible.

Chapter 3: The Price of a Password

"Be careful about reading health books. You may die of a misprint"

-Mark Twain

Analogy

Imagine you're the warden of a high-security prison. Top-notch cameras, well-trained guards, constant monitoring - everything's in place to keep the prison secure. You have total visibility, but then you head out to a social event but forgot to take the prison keys out of your pocket. The keys slip out while you're busy mingling at the social event. Someone else gets hold of them and frees all the inmates. Let's say you have a well-protected house, but the cleaning company that you parted ways with still has the keys. Theoretically, they can still break in because you didn't change the lock. That's the simplicity of a credential-based attack. It bypasses all your security – firewalls, anti-malware, security patches. Your kingdom is well-protected, but the intruder holds the keys.

Breach Data

Despite all the progress we have made in cybersecurity, the Verizon 2025 Data Breach Investigations Report confirms that insecure credentials continue to be our weakest point, our Achilles' heel. Credential abuse was the leading initial access vector in 22% of all breaches. 88% of basic web application attacks involved stolen credentials. Infostealers, a type of malware that silently harvests passwords from browsers, VPNs, and email clients, are fueling this crisis. In the median case, only 49% of a user's passwords across different services were unique, meaning the other half were reused across multiple sites. And here's a sobering detail: only 3% of compromised passwords met basic complexity requirements. We are still losing to the basics.

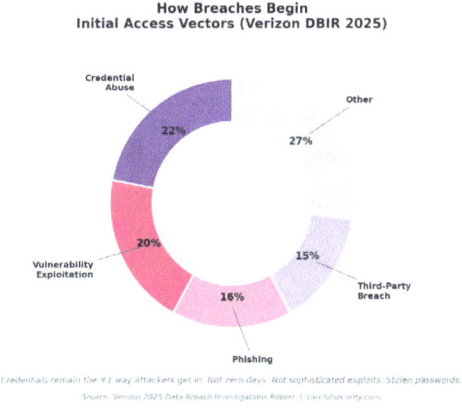

Tracing back to the origin

Data in the dark web

During their cyber attack of 2021, Colonial Pipeline had to shut down its operations for several days, leading to panic buying and long lines at gas stations. The impact of the attack rippled across the East Coast of the United States. Gas prices surged, long lines formed at gas stations, and several states had to declare states of emergency. The company paid a ransom of $4.4 million in Bitcoin to regain access to its systems. Would you believe that it all started with a single compromised password of a former employee? The attackers got hold of the employee's VPN account in a credential dump on the dark web. The account was still active and connecting to the corporate VPN didn't require MFA. Once they got in, the attackers were able to laterally move inside the flat network that wasn't segmented and exploited the security vulnerabilities that were not patched. The attack pointed out multiple gaps in Colonial Pipeline's infrastructure but it all started with a single compromised password.

Password Thieves

Attackers use sneaky tricks to steal your passwords and usernames. They might send you a fake login page that looks just like your work email or bank website. It's designed to trick you into typing in your real information. They can also install malware on your computer. This nasty software records everything you type, including your passwords, and sends it straight to the attacker. If your website or account isn't protected by something called "multi-factor authentication", attackers can use brute force. They'll try tons of different username and password combinations until they find one that works. To prevent this, configure your authentication process to lock out accounts after a certain number of failed attempts.

Artificial intelligence has changed the economics of credential theft. AI-powered tools can generate personalized phishing emails in seconds that are nearly indistinguishable from legitimate messages. Voice deepfakes impersonate executives and IT staff to trick employees into resetting passwords over the phone. This is exactly how the MGM Resorts breach happened in 2023. Automated credential stuffing tools powered by AI adapt in real time, testing stolen username and password combinations across thousands of sites simultaneously, adjusting their patterns to evade detection. The Verizon 2025 DBIR found that AI-crafted malicious emails have doubled over the past two years. And with infostealers harvesting credentials silently in the background, attackers often have your password before you even know it was stolen. One infostealer called Lumma infected over 394,000 Windows devices worldwide before law enforcement shut it down in 2025.

Password Cracking Tool

Attackers are constantly scouring breach data in the dark web for leaked passwords from sites that have been hacked. If you used the same password on multiple sites, and one of the sites get breached, all your other accounts are at risk too. The attackers will try to log in everywhere with your stolen information. All of this is done with automated tools, so it's not like they're manually entering every password. Password-cracking tools use a dictionary-based word and combine it numbers and symbols to imitate the complexity of a real-world password

Organizational Realities

Reluctance to change

We had somewhat of a rebel employee who resented changing passwords every 6 months as dictated by the corporate policy. The password policy states that you cannot use any of the last 10 passwords. So, he kept adding one additional character to his "new" password and changed it ten times until he could revert to his original password.

Sharing is not Caring

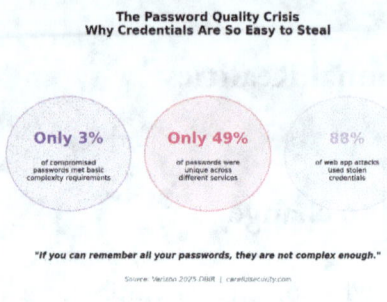

Password123

Sharing passwords, even with trusted individuals, significantly increases the risk of unauthorized access and data breaches. When a password is shared, it's no longer under the sole control of the original owner. If one of the owners leaves the organization or exposes it inadvertently through insecure sharing practices, the shared accounts become vulnerable. Tracking who accessed what information becomes complicated, making audits and investigations more challenging.

Enduring service accounts

Service accounts are behind the scenes accounts that run critical business applications and systems. We've worked with organizations that haven't changed their service account passwords in over a decade. No one wants to change it fearing that it will make critical systems collapse. As a result, they often have elevated privileges and long lifespans. Attackers leverage the longevity of a weak service account passwords to gain a foothold in the network. To mitigate risks associated with stale service account passwords, we have to identify the dependencies first. Then we rotate the passwords in a test environment. Implementing externalized tools can streamline the process of password changes and reduce reliance on manual intervention. We should monitor service account activity for indications of compromise or misuse. Implementing least privilege principles, where service accounts are only granted the minimum necessary permissions, would limit the impact of a potential breach. Consider externalizing service account passwords in independent configuration systems instead of burying it deep in the code.

Remote Access

Many organizations provide remote access to third parties for remote support purposes. However, password is often shared among multiple people and as a result the account is not locked down with MFA. This can create a vulnerable pathway into the corporate network. Securing remote access for third parties is like being a good host: you want to welcome your guests, but also protect your home. Require a strong VPN for a secure connection, then add MFA individual account protection. Inside, give them role based access only to the rooms they need and segment your network to keep sensitive areas separate.

Third-party credential risk expanded dramatically in 2025. The Verizon DBIR reported that breaches involving external partners doubled year over year, now accounting for 30% of all breaches, up from 15% in 2024. These weren't limited to software supply chain vulnerabilities. They included credential exposures from partners, misconfigured SaaS environments, and a lack of secure-by-default settings. The Snowflake breach was a defining example: approximately 80% of the compromised accounts had prior credential exposure, potentially collected by infostealers. Over 100 companies were affected because they did not require multi-factor authentication for account access. A basic control that could have prevented the entire incident.

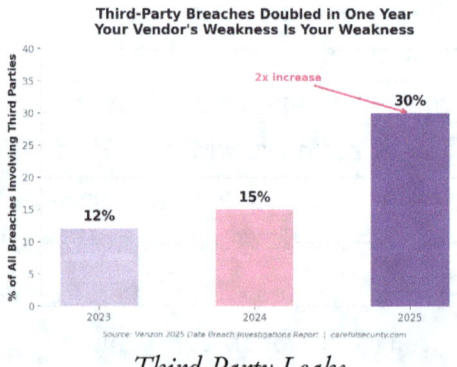

Third Party Leaks

Reusing Corporate Passwords

Reusing corporate passwords for personal accounts is like using the same key for your home, office, and gym locker. If you lose your keys in the gym, you expose home and office premises as well. Similarly, when a cybercriminal manages to compromise one of your personal accounts, they could potentially gain access to your corporate network. This practice, unfortunately, is quite common, as people often prioritize convenience over security.

The problem extends beyond password reuse to where those passwords live. The Verizon 2025 DBIR found that 46% of compromised systems were unmanaged devices, likely personal laptops and phones outside IT's control. These devices stored both personal and corporate login credentials. Among organizations hit with ransomware, 54% had their domains appear in credential dumps, and 40% had corporate email addresses leaked alongside them. Access brokers are using these stolen credentials to sell ready-made entry points to ransomware operators. Your employee's personal laptop, with your corporate password saved in the browser, is an open door you may not know exists.

Mixed Feelings Multi-factor

Multi-factor authentication has been in the news. You may have been reminded about it by IT professionals. It may be a spot of bother or a pet peeve that interrupts your busy flow of activities. As shown in the above screenshot from the password cracking tool passwords are very easy to break by using a combination of known disclosed passwords. If passwords work based on what you know, multi-factor authentication is based on what you have. Bio-metrics work based on what you are. Try not to use SMS or text-based messaging as your second factor of authentication unless you have to, they are susceptible to SIM-swapping attacks. Use an authenticator app like Google Authenticator as your second factor. If you use a password manager, you can integrate your authenticator app seamlessly so you don't have to look into your phone for a code.

 The industry is moving toward eliminating passwords entirely. FIDO2 passkeys use cryptographic keys stored on your device instead of passwords. They cannot be phished, reused across domains, or intercepted by infostealers. Google reports over 400 million accounts now use passkeys. Unlike traditional MFA that can be bypassed through token theft, SIM swapping, or prompt bombing (flooding the user with push notifications until they accept one out of frustration), passkeys are resistant to all of these techniques. The Verizon 2025 DBIR documented a surge in MFA bypass methods, reinforcing the case that not all MFA is equal. If your organization hasn't started evaluating passkeys, it should. They represent the strongest available defense against credential-based attacks, which remain the number one way breaches begin.

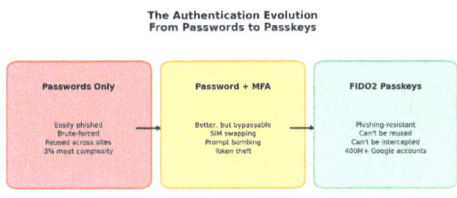

From Passwords to Passkeys

The golden rule is that if a link is publicly accessible on the internet it should have multi-factor authentication. Ideally, it should be prioritized based on the sensitivity of the information, but if the site doesn't support MFA, you should have a long and complex password that's much harder to brute-force. If you remember your passwords, you're doing it wrong. If you can remember all of your passwords chances are that they are not complex enough. All you need to remember is the master password for your password manager and the login password to your workstation. This should include RDP-based access as they are one of the most commonly targeted attack vectors. Single Sign-On also makes password management much easier, and user onboarding and off-boarding easier. For example, if someone leaves the organization, you don't have to go and remove their accounts separately in VPN, SaaS Apps,

File Sharing platforms, etc. Just deactivate one single account in the user workspace and it takes care of deactivating all the linked account accesses.

Default Passwords

Changing default passwords is part of the security hardening process. Most vendors are trying to do away with default passwords, but if you still have a login portal with a default user name and password or a weak password for your home router or IoT smart device, for your audio-visual systems make sure you have a process in place to change that. We have conducted many penetration testing exercises where our job was made much easier because of these default passwords. Attackers love those default passwords, they are low-hanging fruits.

Cloud Infrastructure Passwords

We notice that multi-factor authentication isn't always used for important accounts on Amazon Web Services (AWS). There have been incidents in the past where a cyber-attacker exploited the lack of Multi-Factor on the AWS cloud infrastructure of a well known company at that time. They broke into AWS and deleted their entire cloud infrastructure. The company in question didn't have offline immutable backups and had to shut down their entire business overnight.

A newer risk emerged in 2025 that didn't exist when we wrote the first edition: employees using AI tools with corporate credentials. The Verizon 2025 DBIR found that 15% of employees access generative AI platforms from corporate devices every couple of weeks. 72% of them use personal email accounts to do it, and 17% use corporate emails that aren't protected by SSO or SAML. Every time an employee pastes corporate data into an AI tool authenticated with a personal account, that data leaves your security perimeter. Shadow AI is the new shadow IT, and it's happening with your credentials.

Tools, Resources & Solutions

Change your credentials regularly, use strong authentication, and keep an eye on the dark web to make sure they haven't been leaked. Organizations should scour the Internet and dark web to discover if their organizational passwords have been breached. Some password managers provide this feature. You can also use tools like DeHashed or security researcher Troy Hunt's 'Have I Been Pwned'[1] tool to detect if your password has been compromised.

---

1. https://haveibeenpwned.com/

If you notice that your password has been compromised change it and don't reuse it.

Periodic Access Reviews

When we conduct access reviews for our clients we notice forgotten accounts that are still active. People change organizations, projects are closed, and departments evolve yet the old accounts survive through all the turmoils. When we fail to remove accounts in due time we lose track of who was using it especially if it wasn't documented. Dormant accounts, like forgotten keys, represent potential vulnerabilities that attackers can exploit. By reviewing access rights and disabling unused accounts every quarter, we make it harder for attackers to gain unauthorized access.

Password Managers

It is not enough to ask the user to change their passwords. We should offer them a mechanism to save it securely. Enter password management solutions. They automate password generation, autofill passwords, integrate MFA seamlessly, and allow secure sharing in a vault. We need to take the time to educate our users on the usage and adoption of password managers. It will increase adoption. Some people are skeptical of storing all their passwords in a manager as it may create a single point of failure similar to keeping all your eggs in one basket. We should enquire with them about the alternatives in such scenarios.

Password Vaults

Instead of sharing passwords, we can use shared vaults within the password manager. It allows easy rotation of passwords and provides a secure sharing mechanism by adding or removing users from a shared vault. Access can be granted or revoked granularly, ensuring that only authorized individuals have the necessary permissions. It also logs user activity and increases auditability by tracking who used the shared password.

Privileged Account Management Tools

Administrators should consider using two separate accounts. One is your regular user account, and then you have your privileged administrative account. Think about them as the master keys that open every room in the hotel. So they should be handled with extra caution. Use a YubiKey or similar hardware-based multi-factor authentication to restrict access to authorized devices only. Privileged access management should also be logged. Once the attacker breaks in with a regular user account, they try to elevate their privilege to become an admin account.

What This Means For Your Business

Credentials remain the number one way breaches begin. Not zero-day exploits. Not nation-state hackers. Stolen, weak, and reused passwords. The Verizon 2025 DBIR found that 88% of basic web application attacks involved stolen credentials, and only 3% of compromised passwords met basic complexity requirements. The fixes are not expensive: deploy multi-factor authentication on every publicly accessible system, implement a password manager for your team, run quarterly access reviews to catch dormant accounts, and start evaluating passkeys as the next generation of authentication. If your organization has remote access portals, cloud infrastructure, or third-party vendor connections without MFA, you have an open door. The attackers already know it's there. Close it before they walk through.

Chapter 4: Distributed Data

"The things that you own end up owing you."

-Chuck Palahniuk, Fight Club

When we were moving from the East Coast to the Midwest, we paid the movers five thousand dollars for moving busted mattresses and battered furniture, which didn't cost that much in the first place. We could have saved some of the money and bought new furniture instead. Hindsight 20-20. Needless to say, like most husbands, I didn't have a say in such matters. Do we hang on to our data for the sake of nostalgia and memory? How do we reduce our ownership in the information age? Can we delete the data we don't need? It's worth the effort as we will save money, and storage space and reduce the attack surface.

Location of Breached Data

Where your data lives directly determine how much a breach costs. The IBM 2025 Cost of a Data Breach Report found that breaches involving data stored across multiple environments cost an average of $5.05 million and took 276 days to identify and contain. That's 59 days longer and over a million dollars more than breaches involving data stored in a single on-premises environment. The pattern is clear: as data sprawls across more platforms, security teams lose visibility and control, leading to longer exposure periods and higher costs. 30% of all breaches in 2025 involved data distributed across multiple environments. Multiple data repositories expand the potential entry points for unauthorized access and cyberattacks. Tracking data across repositories can be challenging with Shadow IT's usage of unsanctioned cloud services, creating additional data repositories outside organizational control.

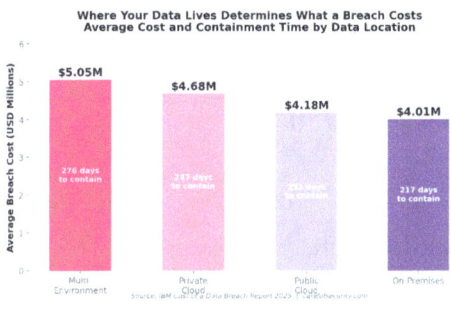

Data Everywhere

Attackers are motivated by financial gain, disruption, or political and ideological reasons. All organizations must recognize their potential as targets and implement strong cybersecurity measures starting with attack surface management to monitor their security exposures. Any organization, regardless of size or perceived data value, can be a victim of cyberattacks.

MITRE ATT&CK Framework

The MITRE ATT&CK framework is like a detailed guidebook that explains all the different attack paths adversaries can use to break into our organizations. It demonstrates the different techniques adversaries may attempt to get a foothold, gain access, evade detection, and launch attacks. By studying this guidebook, we can understand cyber-attack tactics and implement stronger security measures to limit the damage and facilitate quick responses.

AT&T Data Breach

In 2023 AT&T discovered a 2023 data breach at one of its cloud vendors. The breach exposed information like the number of lines on an account and, in some cases, bill balances and rate plans for 8.9 million AT&T wireless customers. The exposed data was from 2015-2017 and should have been deleted years ago. The data was stored within, a third-party cloud vendor. The incident brought attention to the potential dangers of a distributed data environment and the storage of sensitive customer information with external vendors. Companies need to make sure that they protect their data, even when it's being handled by third-party systems.

AT&T was hit again in 2024 when hackers accessed call and text records of nearly all of its wireless customers through a third-party cloud platform. Attackers obtained login credentials through infostealer malware and used them to access AT&T's Snowflake environment, which lacked multi-factor authentication. A username and password were all it took. Two breaches, two different failure modes. The first was a data retention failure: data that should have been deleted sat in a vendor environment for years. The second was a credential hygiene failure: stolen passwords with no MFA. Both trace back to the same underlying gap: insufficient controls over sensitive data in third-party environments.

Organizational Realities

Shadow IT

Shadow data refers to the unauthorized storage and use of data by employees or third-party entities. It increases the difficulty of tracking and safeguarding data. When users decide to manage their own IT needs, they sign up for third-party applications and services without going through an IT Security review. It increases the footprint of distributed data and decentralizes data management and governance practices. Shadow data is often forgotten and hard-to-track and data. It accounts for almost one third of data breaches, and when it's stolen, the cost of the breach goes up significantly. It turns out that almost one in two organizations is storing data in multiple places: a mix of public cloud, on-premises servers, and private clouds.

The IBM 2025 report found that 20% of breaches were linked to shadow AI, where employees use unsanctioned AI tools without IT oversight. Customer PII was compromised in 65% of shadow AI breaches. Intellectual property exposure jumped to 40%. The average enterprise now hosts approximately 1,200 unofficial applications, and most organizations are completely blind to their AI data flows. Every time an employee pastes customer data, financial records, or internal communications into an AI tool, that data leaves your security perimeter. And unlike traditional shadow IT, where the data stays on a server somewhere, data shared with AI models becomes embedded in ways that may be impossible to reverse. Only a small subsection of the organizations conducted regular audits to detect unsanctioned AI usage while most of the organizations had no AI governance policies.

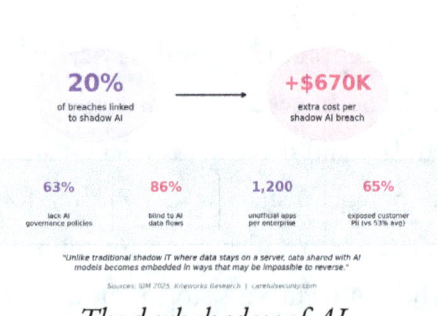

The dark shadow of AI

Data Risk Assessment

We recently assessed a health and wellness institute with a massive database. Millions of membership records date back 30 years, while their current membership was only in hundreds of thousands. This old data was a burden, slowing down their systems and increasing maintenance costs. Plus, with all that personal information, the fines for a data breach could be astronomical. We asked why they kept this risky data. They mentioned a few fringe cases, like tracking members with past payment issues. Fair enough, but why keep everything else? Hopefully, they can take our advice and remove unnecessary historical data. But change isn't easy. Their marketing team might push back, wanting to keep everything for campaigns. If marketing won't budge, would they accept the risk of a breach? Or would they blame IT security for the massive fines from a regulatory data breach? IT security shouldn't have to make business calls. Present the facts to management, so they understand the consequences and limitations. Let's also try to minimize sensitive data. Do we need all the detailed historical health records? Would names and emails be just fine for future email campaigns? Reduce sensitive data to reduce the burden of compliance.

Digital Hoarding

There's a natural tendency to hold on to our data. The consequences of not deleting data include non-compliance with regulatory data privacy requirements. Do we hang on to our data for the sake of nostalgia and memory? Finding the data to delete is like searching for a needle in a haystack. Data is scattered across different systems, and without a clear map, it's tough to even know where to start. There's always that nagging fear of accidentally deleting something important. Regulations around data deletion are often vague and confusing, leaving organizations unsure of what to keep and when to delete it. It's like following a recipe with missing ingredients and unclear instructions. Then there are internal struggles. Some folks worry that deleting data too soon could hinder innovation or erase valuable company history. Data deletion is complex, time-consuming, and fraught with risks. No wonder many organizations keep postponing the deletion of data instead of tackling the cleanup.

A less visible but increasingly critical risk is what happens to data during migration. As organizations move from legacy systems to cloud platforms, implement AI pipelines, or consolidate after mergers and acquisitions, large volumes of sensitive data move between environments. IBM's 2025 report found that poorly managed data movement during system upgrades, cloud adoption, or AI implementation is a recurring factor in breaches. Data gets copied to staging environments that lack production-level security controls. Temporary storage locations become permanent. Access permissions set during migration never get reverted to least privilege. If you don't know what you're moving, where it's going, and who has the keys, you're creating risk with every transfer.

Data Discovery

Organizations face challenges when discovering and categorizing their data. The data is vast and varied, including files, emails, databases, and more, all in different formats. Data silos across different departments make it difficult to get a complete picture. We don't know who is responsible for what data and that creates orphan data with no ownership. Many organizations don't have automated processes for data discovery and classification. New data gets introduced and the way people use data evolves. To avoid data breaches and regulatory fines, we must know what sensitive data we house and where it's located. Once data is discovered, we need to ensure access is restricted based on business needs only.

Data Leakage

Data leakage is the unauthorized transmission or exposure of sensitive or confidential data from within an organization. Data Leakage can take place through misconfigured systems, improperly configured databases, cloud storage, or file-sharing services that allow unauthorized access. It can take place through human error when we send data to the wrong recipient, accidentally post information publicly, or lose devices containing sensitive data. Intentional Leaks take place through disgruntled employees or contractors disclosing data for financial gain or to harm the organization. It can take place through insecure disposal of equipment, for example through old hard drives or devices that contain data that has not been properly wiped before disposal. It can take place through third-party breaches when data is entrusted to partners or vendors who get compromised. It can occur because of inadequate data access controls where employees have access to more data than they need to perform their jobs. Employees may move sensitive corporate data to their personal devices, either accidentally or intentionally. IT departments have limited visibility and control over personal devices. Lost or stolen devices have exposed confidential company data in the past.

The Verizon 2025 DBIR found that employees access generative AI platforms from corporate devices regularly. Some of them authenticate with personal email accounts. Some use corporate emails without SSO or SAML protection. When employees paste sensitive data into AI chatbots, upload documents to AI summarization tools, or input customer records into AI-powered analytics, that data may be used to train models, stored in environments you don't control, or exposed through API vulnerabilities. IBM found that 83% of organizations lack technical controls to detect or prevent employees from uploading confidential data to AI platforms. It's happening across every industry and across every company size.

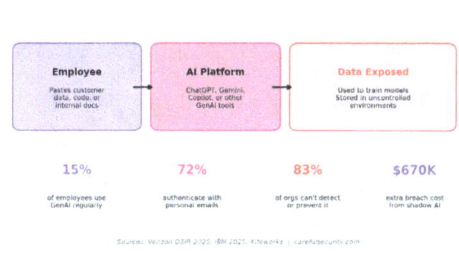

AI knows it all

Excess Access

With excess access, employees might stumble upon sensitive data they shouldn't see, like customer lists or secret company recipes. Sometimes we allow third-party vendors way more access than they need. Even development environments can be a problem. They're often set up to be just like the live environment, which means developers and admins have access to live data. Some departments store data in their own silos with no centralized governance. There seems to be too much access with too little oversight.

Tools, Resources, Solutions

User Education

Educate your staff on best practices for handling data and the risks that come with it. Make sure you can recover your data from your backups. Track how data moves within and out of your organization. Restrict how vendors and third-party partners access your data. Data leakage can lead to fines, loss of trust, and lost contracts.

Creating a Data Retention Policy

Ensure that our retention schedules are visible to everyone. We need data governance and cybersecurity frameworks to work together effectively. The key is to keep the policy simple and ensure that everyone understands it. Establishing effective data retention policies requires the participation of legal, IT, compliance, and business units. It can be challenging to align everyone due to their differing priorities. Our policies must ensure that we can access data for business or legal purposes while safeguarding sensitive information from unauthorized access and breaches. It may require some effort, but it will save money and storage space and reduce risk in the long run. Data retention rules vary depending on the industry, location, and type of data. Figuring out how long to keep different types of data can be a challenge. Before spending money on specialized tools, we must explore the native functionalities of Office 365 and Google Workspace. People don't always know who owns what, and IT and leadership need to work together on this. Keep the policy simple and make sure everyone understands it.

Data Retention

Different data types have unique values. Retention schedules should be published internally for everyone's knowledge. Ensure that we have proper authorization before conducting data discovery. Take a process-oriented approach rather than solely relying on tools. Integrate your data governance practices with cybersecurity frameworks like NIST CSF. Explore native functionalities in Office

365 and Google Workspace before purchasing specialized tools. Data Duplication: Companies may also end up with the same data in multiple locations. For e.g. employees may copy the same data from one SharePoint location to a Dropbox location to share with a client. As a company matures, it moves from data disengaged to data enabled, to data driven. The data management program is multi-faceted with strategy, architecture, operations, and risk management.

The Principle of Least Privilege

Cybersecurity best practices require that access should be granted on a "need-to-know" basis. This means providing individuals with only the permissions necessary to perform their specific job functions. Restricting access in this way limits the potential damage in the event of a security incident or unauthorized access. Creating role-based access control across the organization starts with mapping which role needs what access to which systems. Once that is decided and signed by all stakeholders, the principle of least privilege can be set in motion.

Data Loss Prevention

Deploy security measures like access policies and data loss prevention tools across all repositories. Conduct periodic data audits to identify risks and vulnerabilities and implement continuous monitoring to identify security anomalies. Classify data based on sensitivity and implement appropriate access controls to ensure only authorized personnel can access sensitive data. Implement policies for data retention, archiving, and deletion to ensure compliance and minimize storage costs.

Browser Tracking

With browser tracking tools, organizations can monitor the websites and services employees use for sensitive data. It can identify the usage of cloud storage services, collaboration platforms, and even third-party vendor portals. By creating browser policies, we can identify where sensitive data is being uploaded or shared and monitor data entry in unauthorized platforms. Understanding where employees upload or share data helps build a more accurate data map. Browser tracking helps flag when employees may be using unapproved services that could lead to potential data leaks or non-compliance with company policies.

NIST Privacy Framework

The NIST Privacy Framework provides a toolbox for building a strong privacy program. It helps organizations manage risks, build trust, and follow the rules, all while adapting to your specific needs. It can be adopted by organizations to establish a step-by-step guide to managing privacy risks as it helps you figure out where the risks are, how to protect against them, and what to do if something goes wrong. The framework aids in identifying privacy issues and promotes transparency regarding data collection and usage. Privacy requires continuous effort and should not be treated as a one-time task.

The framework was updated in 2024 with additional guidance on AI and machine learning data governance, reflecting the growing recognition that privacy frameworks must evolve alongside the technologies they govern.

IAPP

The IAPP is a global, non-profit organization focused on defining, promoting, and improving the privacy profession. While primarily concerned with privacy, the IAPP's resources and expertise can also help organizations improve their cybersecurity programs. They help drive home the point that we can't have privacy without the security component and vice versa. Like peanut butter and jelly, they go together. IAPP offers training and certifications and case studies on how to bake privacy into our security plan and keeps us updated with the privacy laws and best practices.

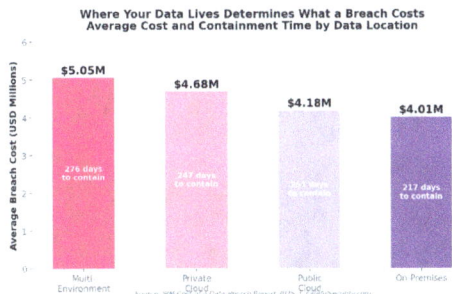

Price of lost data

What This Means for Your Business

Data you don't need is a liability you're paying to store and protect. Breaches involving data spread across multiple environments cost $5.05 million, over a million dollars more than single-environment breaches. Shadow AI breaches cost $670,000 more than standard incidents, and 86% of organizations can't even see where their AI data flows. The practical steps: conduct data inventory to know what you have and where it lives. Apply retention policies to delete what you no longer need. Classify what remains at a sensitivity level. Restrict access to the minimum necessary for each role. Monitor for shadow AI usage and establish clear policies before your employees create the problem for you. And if you're planning a migration to the cloud or implementing AI tools, build security into the migration plan from day one, not after the data has already moved. The moving truck story at the beginning of this chapter happens more often than you think. It's the most expensive mistake most organizations make with their data.

Chapter 5: Security Skills Shortage

DIY Project Gone Wrong

"Alone, we can do so little; together, we can do so much."

-Helen Keller

We live in an older house that needs occasional upgrades and replacements. Our kitchen sink was clogging up every other month. We thought we knew enough about kitchen sinks to fix the problem ourselves. First, we tried applying all sorts of chemicals that seemed to work very slowly. Then we ordered special plungers to expedite the process. Even though they worked, they were more of a temporary fix and we had to repeat the same process every other month. We tried taking out the sink and putting in a new one, but we couldn't get the old sink removed! It was rattled and refused to budge. Then we got distracted, we thought, "Instead of replacing it, why don't we just paint and repair the surface to make it look new? We'll save money, get the look we want, and remove those old worn-out tear marks. We put on layer after layer of paint, maybe a few too many, and the sink ended up looking worse than before, all battered and bruised. Finally, we came to our senses and decided to call a professional. The professional was able to take out the old sink, put in a new one, and even fix the broken plumbing we didn't know we had. Now our sink doesn't clog up every other month! Sure, we had to pay a bit more for the professional help, but now we don't worry about our kitchen sink clogs anymore. Anyone else had a similar experience?

The ISC2 2025 Cybersecurity Workforce Study confirms what every hiring manager already knows: the shortage is getting more complicated. The global cybersecurity workforce stands at approximately 5.5 million professionals, with an estimated 4.8 million unfilled positions worldwide. CyberSeek reports over 500,000 open positions in the United States alone.

But the 2025 study revealed something new: the problem is shifting from headcount to skills. Cybersecurity professionals said the need for critical skills within the workforce outweighs the need to increase headcount. This trend emerged in 2024 and became the dominant finding in 2025. You can hire more people, but if they don't have the right skills, particularly in AI security, cloud security, and incident response, the gap doesn't close.

88% of organizations reported at least one significant cybersecurity event in the past year because of skills shortages. Budget is the primary barrier: 33% of organizations don't have the resources to staff their teams adequately, and 29% can't afford to hire staff with the skills they need.

Shifting Demand

The financial cost of understaffing is measurable. Organizations with high-level security staffing shortages paid an average of $1.76 million more per breach than adequately staffed organizations. The problem hits small businesses harder. According to the Identity Theft Resource Center's 2025 Business Impact Report, 81% of small businesses reported suffering a security breach, a data breach, or both in the prior 12 months. AI-powered attacks were identified as a believed root cause in more than 40% of those events. Among breached small businesses, 62.5% reported a total financial impact exceeding $250,000, and more than a third faced costs above $500,000. To pay for recovery, 38.3% of small business leaders reported for the first time that they raised prices, creating a hidden "cyber tax" passed on to customers. Even though SMB leadership wants to believe they're not important enough to be a target, the 2025 Verizon Data Breach Investigations Report found that SMBs are targeted nearly four times more than large organizations, with ransomware present in 88% of SMB breaches compared to just 39% at enterprise-sized firms.

Cybercriminals are aware that SMBs often ignore their cybersecurity needs. They also know smaller businesses have access to sensitive information of customers and clients. In their mind, SMBs are easy targets because they don't have the money, tools, tech, or skilled people to really protect themselves. They may make a business decision that it's easier to hack three weak targets than a resourceful one. They may not make the headlines because they're smaller in size, but that doesn't mean they aren't getting targeted.

The percentage of small business leaders who feel "very prepared" for a cyberattack is dropping. Despite the heightened risks, the implementation of basic security measures is declining. Businesses know the threats are growing. They're just not doing the basics to protect themselves. [1]

---

1. https://www.insurancebusinessmag.com/us/news/cyber/despite-awareness-small-businesses-still-highly-vulnerable-to-cyber-attacks-474678.aspx

Organizational Realities

Defenders of the castle

Cybersecurity Barrier to Entry

When people talk about the "cybersecurity barrier to entry," they mean all the obstacles that make it hard to get started in this field. For one thing, there's no single, straightforward path to a cybersecurity career, which can be pretty confusing. Companies are always looking for people with the right skills, both technical know-how and the ability to work well with others. If you're new to the field, it's definitely a challenge to break in. There is also a lack of diversity. The industry needs more women and minorities, and the current lack of representation makes it even harder for those groups to get involved. On top of that, cybersecurity education and certifications can be expensive, so not everyone can afford the training they need.

Even for professionals who make it past the barrier to entry, the industry is burning them out. The ISC2 2025 study found that 48% of cybersecurity professionals feel exhausted from trying to stay current on the latest threats and emerging technologies. 47% feel overwhelmed by workload.

Job satisfaction has declined for three consecutive years: 74% in 2022, 70% in 2023, 66% in 2024. The people doing this work are less happy every year, and the economic pressures are making it worse. 24% experienced layoffs on their teams. 36% experienced budget cuts. 38% faced hiring freezes. The largest organizations were hit hardest, with 32% reporting layoffs, 46% budget cuts, 49% hiring freezes, and 41% promotion freezes.

Only 34% of respondents said they have the right level of cybersecurity staffing. We have a field that is simultaneously understaffed and burning out the people it does have. That is not a pipeline problem. That is a systemic problem.

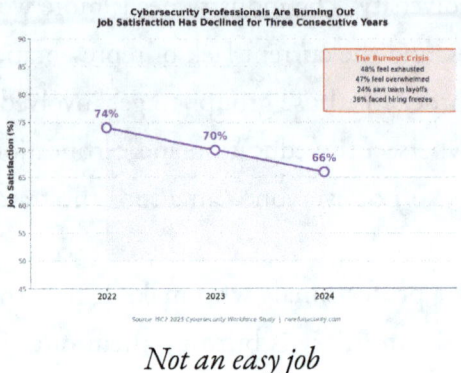

Not an easy job

Career Pathways

Aspiring cybersecurity professionals should be realistic about their career paths. The field of cybersecurity presents many career opportunities, encompassing a diverse array of paths. They span from technical positions like penetration testers and SOC analysts to relatively non-technical roles like security compliance specialists. Starting in a compliance role and gradually transitioning to more technical roles like SOC analyst or penetration tester is one way to make a lateral movement after gaining experience and knowledge. New entrants should be aware of these diverse options and not limit themselves to the romanticized image of a "hacker." A successful cybersecurity career spans a gradual progression of skills and responsibilities. Starting in compliance or as a SOC analyst will provide valuable experience and a steppingstone toward a more technical role if that is of interest. As expertise grows, professionals should leverage their knowledge to influence organizational change and improve security practices.

According to CyberSeek, the joint NIST/CompTIA/Lightcast initiative, the United States currently has over 470,000 open cybersecurity positions. The supply-demand ratio confirms chronic undersupply, with the gap widest in Virginia, Maryland, and the D.C. metro area where federal demand concentrates. On average, cybersecurity roles take 21% longer to fill than other IT jobs. And 89% of hiring managers will not consider candidates without at least one cybersecurity certification, a hard filter that operates before a resume reaches a human reviewer. Yet three of the top five skills hiring managers value most are not technical at all: teamwork, problem-solving, and analytical thinking. The industry says it needs more technical people but actually needs more people who can think, communicate, and collaborate while also understanding technology.

Cybersecurity Gold Rush

The California gold rush began on January 24, 1848, when gold was found by James W. Marshall at Sutter's Mill in Coloma, California. The news of gold brought approximately 300,000 people to California from the rest of the

United States and abroad. Are we going through a similar gold rush where many people are joining cybersecurity in the search of a lucrative career. Would the adoption of AI help bridge this gap?

The answer is: partially, but not the way most people expect. AI is reshaping cybersecurity roles rather than replacing them. The ISC2 2025 study found that many professionals believe that AI will create more specialized cybersecurity skill requirements, will necessitate more strategic mindsets, and require broader skillsets across the workforce. AI is the number one skill gap followed by cloud security. Cybersecurity professionals are already working to gain AI knowledge and skills and pursue AI qualifications. The professionals who learn to work alongside AI, using it for threat detection, automated response, and behavioral analysis while applying human judgment to the results, will be dramatically more valuable than those who treat AI as either a threat or a savior. The gold rush isn't over. But the gold has moved. From learning about firewalls and subnets to understanding how AI changes both the attack surface and the defense.

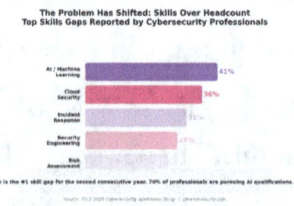

Cybersecurity Academies

The need for hands on tinkering

The need for hands on tinkering

Cybersecurity Academies are booming, promising lucrative careers after short boot camps. However, their success rate is often inflated. The few graduates who land jobs do so primarily due to their pre-existing passion and self-driven learning, not solely because of the academy's training program. Many cybersecurity instructors lack real-life corporate experience. They rely heavily on the theoretical mode of training-based OSI Models. This creates a disconnect between academia and industry, resulting in a gap in practical skills. As a result, graduates are unprepared for real-world challenges. Trycyber.us is a free resource provided by the NICE Framework to sharpen your hands-on skills. While multiple-choice tests might demonstrate theoretical knowledge, they don't guarantee real-world success. Cybersecurity requires understanding nuances and adapting to unique situations, something that is often missing from academic settings. Passing tests doesn't guarantee real-world success. Cybersecurity requires critical thinking, problem-solving, and the ability to adapt to complex and ever-changing situations.

Cybersecurity academies should focus on hands-on experience and real-world scenarios, rather than just theoretical concepts. Real-world cybersecurity is more than just running exploits and gaining remote access. It involves understanding the risks of bringing down live environments or introducing malware. Classroom environments should teach students how to handle vulnerabilities in a production environment without causing harm or disruption. Effective training should focus on hands-on experience and address real-world problems. SANS and OSCP, TryHackme and LetsDefend all provide useful hands-on learning experiences. In theory, every organization will maintain perfectly updated systems, follow best practices, and have ample resources for security. Real-life challenges often deviate from this ideal scenario. There are budget constraints, resource limitations, and competing priorities. Developing these insights is crucial for promoting security improvements and bringing about change within an organization.

Specialization or Generalization

Instead of trying to cover every aspect of cybersecurity, academies should encourage students to specialize in a specific area, such as penetration testing, Security Operation Center Analysts, or Governance, Risk, and Compliance specialists. This allows career aspirants to develop expertise in their chosen field. A well-rounded cybersecurity professional can have real-world experience of spotting attack patterns, repeating those patterns to break into systems, and influencing change by establishing security best practices. It would allow them to have a deeper understanding of how attackers operate and how to defend against them.

The ISC2 2025 Hiring Trends study revealed something the industry needs to hear: hiring managers are setting unrealistic expectations for entry-level candidates, creating a barrier that discourages otherwise qualified people from applying. The study recommends hiring attitude and training for aptitude, embracing alternative pathways including internships, apprenticeships, and non-traditional backgrounds. Organizations should expand their definition of what a "qualified" cybersecurity candidate looks like. The best security teams we've worked with include former teachers, military veterans, accountants, and musicians. Diverse backgrounds create diverse thinking, and diverse thinking catch threats that homogeneous teams miss.

Tools, Resources, and Solutions

Career Options

The [2] NICE Framework provides a map of different career paths you can take. It's broken down into seven categories, and each one has entry-level jobs you could aim for. You can use it to find the best match for your skills and what you're interested in. For example, if you're interested in the big-picture stuff, you could look into Oversight and Governance roles. You might start by helping out with creating cybersecurity policies or doing some legal research. If you're more technical, design and development might be your thing. Think about learning secure coding practices or testing new systems. There's also Implementation and Operation, where you'd be keeping systems up and running securely. If you like the idea of fighting off attacks, check out Protection and Defense. You could assist with things like risk analysis and figuring out where systems are vulnerable. If you are an aspiring detective, Investigation could be a good fit. You'd be helping gather and ana-

---

2. https://niccs.cisa.gov/workforce-development/nice-framework

lyze digital evidence. There's also Cyberspace Intelligence, where you'd be looking at information about what's happening online. Cyberspace Effects might be a bit trickier to get into at first, but it's something to aim for if you're interested in the strategic side of cybersecurity.

Career Pathway Tools[3]

The NICE Framework has created a shared language for cybersecurity work and skills, so everyone is on the same page. It provides a detailed list of cybersecurity skills to help employers figure out exactly what skills they need and help job seekers understand what different career paths look like. The framework also helps connect education and training programs with what the industry needs, so graduates have the skills employers are looking for. And it even has resources for people to explore cybersecurity careers and figure out what skills they need to develop.

The Unsung Skills of Cybersecurity

It's easy to get caught up in the technical side of cybersecurity: firewalls, intrusion detection, and all that jazz. It's

---

3. https://niccs.cisa.gov/workforce-development/cyber-career-pathways-tool

not just about technology. You need to be able to explain the security risks. You need to be a team player because cybersecurity is a collaborative effort. You also have to be persuasive, because you're a change agent. When things are going wrong, you need to be able to think on your feet and adapt to the situation.

Mentors and Networking

Having a good mentor can completely transform your journey. They can offer guidance, share their experiences, and help you navigate the twists and turns of your career. Don't underestimate the power of networking. Building relationships with other professionals in the field can open doors to new opportunities and provide a valuable support system

Your Community Connection

Joining local security organizations like OWASP, ISSA, or ISACA are fun ways to learn, network, and stay up to date on the latest trends. Plus, it's a chance to meet people in your area who share your passion for cybersecurity. They can help you get connected with potential employers.

Internships: Getting Your Foot in the Door

There's no substitute for real-world experience. An internship can give you a taste of what it's really like to work in cybersecurity and help you build valuable skills. It's also a great way to learn about real-world problems and land a full-time job. Apply for those internship opportunities and gain practical experience.

What This Means for Your Business

The cybersecurity workforce gap isn't closing. If you're a mid-market company competing for cybersecurity talent against enterprises offering higher salaries and better benefits, you have three realistic options. First, outsource the specialized work to a firm that already has expertise. This is what our clients do for security, compliance and daily operations, freeing their teams to focus on building the core business. Second, invest in upskilling your IT team with certifications and hands-on training. Third, consider fractional security leadership through a vCISO arrangement that gives you senior-level expertise without the $250,000+ salary of a full-time hire. What doesn't work: ignoring the problem and hoping your general IT person can handle cybersecurity as a side project. That's the kitchen sink approach, and we already know how that story ends.

Chapter 6: The Art of Simplicity

Too many choices!

"Simplicity is the ultimate sophistication."
-Leonardo da Vinci

Have you ever felt lost in the aisles of a grocery store? I wish they could put a cap on the different kinds of eggs you can sell in one store. White Eggs, Brown Eggs, Nest-Laid Eggs, Free-Run Eggs, Free-Range Eggs, Organic Eggs, Omega-3 Eggs, Pastured Eggs, Vegetarian Eggs. Even before you are done trying them all more choices are added to the list. Farm fresh eggs, locally grown eggs, large brown free-range loose eggs, etc. I almost gave up on buying eggs and bought beer instead.

Security System Complexity

Studies have demonstrated that organizations with overly complex security systems are more susceptible to breaches. Complex systems often have interconnected parts that are difficult to understand and manage. This may result in security misconfiguration, vulnerabilities, and ultimately, security breaches. Prioritizing simplicity in cybersecurity design ensures a more manageable defense and reduces dependence on tribal knowledge. However, achieving simplicity is not always simple.

The IBM 2025 Cost of a Data Breach Report makes the case plainly: complexity kills. Security system complexity remains one of the top cost-amplifying factors behind a data breach. Organizations that consolidated their tools, automated evidence collection, and eliminated redundancy detected breaches faster, contained them quicker, and paid less to recover. The ones that embraced AI and automation in their security operations saved $1.9 million per breach. The difference isn't budget. It's simplicity.

More tools does not equal more security. Subtraction beats addition.[1]

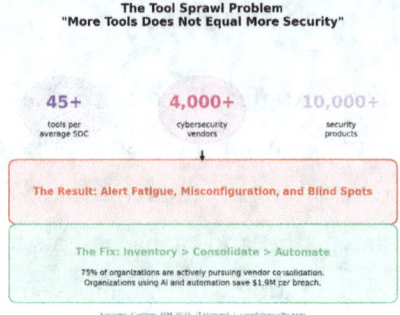

Tool Convergence

Organizational Realities

The number of security providers is mind-boggling. According to the IT-Harvest Dashboard, there are 4,000+ vendors and 10,000+ cybersecurity products ranging from software to hardware.

The average security operations center juggles 45 or more tools. Three out of four organizations are now actively pursuing vendor consolidation. The reason is straightforward: every tool you add requires configuration, maintenance, updates, training, and integration with

---

1. IBM Cost of Data Breach Report 2024

other tools. Each one generates its own alerts. The result is alert fatigue. Security analysts drown in notifications, and the real threats hide in the noise. One of our clients had fourteen security tools and a team of three. They still failed their first SOC 2 readiness assessment. Not because they lacked technology. Because they were drowning in it.[2]

Different wants for different roles

Business owners are responsible for the financial growth of the company. They want solutions that offer a return on investment, help meet regulatory requirements, and keep them out of the news for the wrong reasons. As security professionals, we must help them see a clear correlation between the investment and the ROI. CIOs and CTOs are responsible for managing IT and the technology stack. They are looking for solutions that meet their requirements of easy integration, consistent support, scalability and cost efficiency. They want the tool to be adopted and used by their teams. They are apprehensive of getting locked into vendor contracts that don't deliver on their promises or take far too long to roll out.

CISOs focus on managing and mitigating risks. They seek partners who understand the threat landscape, can

---

2. https://dashboard.it-harvest.com/

help them stay ahead of evolving risks, and offer effective, reliable solutions with actionable insights. They get frustrated by a product that provides false alerts and a fragmented view of their security posture. Marketing buzzwords do not impress them. Give them tools with robust reporting capabilities.

IT and Security teams manage the deployment and management of cybersecurity solutions. They want products that are easy to use and can enhance job efficiency, without requiring extensive learning and offering valuable recommendations. They value vendor responsiveness and knowledge bases. If the product is too complex, it ends up causing them more work. If it takes a long time to deploy and configure, they cannot find the time for it. When they approach the vendor for help, they may get caught in an endless loop of back-and-forth ticketing.

The end users value usability and want to ensure they are complying with security requirements for e.g. MFA, access control, audit logging etc. Companies may sign up for a new tool product or service because the salesperson did a great job of convincing them that the tool is the solution to all their problems, but once the product was purchased, they passed on the responsibility of deploying the tool to the service team who were busy with other deployments.

Companies tend to allocate their best talents selling a product rather than service delivery. Sales teams may make promises that the service team cannot deliver. Once the product is sold the sales team may not show until it's time to renew the contract. They sweeten the deal, make the same promises for version 2.0 all over again, and the tool gets renewed because, well, it's already approved in the budget. We appreciate and remain loyal to vendors who invest in delivery managers that add value to organizations instead of focusing solely on upselling. Customers don't need flashy demos or extensive technical explanations. They are seeking a tool that will provide the assurance to deliver on its promises. I feel strongly on this topic as I have rarely seen the implementation of a product within their promised timelines and that's just unfair.

The Shiny New Toy

Everyone loves a new shiny toy

James Clear, the author of atomic habits, wrote "The greatest threat to success is not failure but boredom. We get bored with habits because they stop delighting us. And as our habits become ordinary, we start derailing our progress to seek novelty."

People in technology like to solve problems. They are also enamored by the idea of new technology and the new shiny toy. It's one of the reasons they got into technology in the first place. We're drawn in by the allure of automation and magical timesavers. The excitement of AI has added fuel to this fire. On the flip side our hastiness to find solutions can lead us to conclusions before we take the time to think through the problem and list all our requirements. Our desire to be the first to come up with a solution can expedite our decision-making. After all, aren't we supposed to be the smartest ones in the room?

AI deserves special mention here because it's the shiniest toy the industry has ever seen. Every vendor now claims their product is "AI-powered." Every conference keynote mentions AI. Every board meeting asks about AI. But the IBM 2025 report tells a cautionary story: the majority of breached organizations lacked AI governance policies entirely, and almost none of those that experienced AI-related security incidents had AI access controls in place. Organizations rushed to deploy AI tools for productivity without asking the basic security questions: What data does this tool access? Where does that data go? Who controls it? Shadow AI became a measurable factor in breaches, adding significant extra costs per incident. AI is a powerful tool when governed properly. When deployed without governance, it's the most expensive shiny toy in the cabinet. Chapter 15 digs deeper into AI governance and ISO 42001, the framework that turns AI from a liability into a competitive advantage.

The Disconnect

Vendors often focus on showcasing the impressive features and capabilities of their tools through demos and marketing materials. However, they rarely address how these tools will function within a potential customer's environment. More time should be spent on understanding the client's infrastructure with all its nuances than sharing what's on display.

Complex Jargons

Security professionals using technical jargon might alienate colleagues from other departments who lack a cybersecurity background. Using technical terms like "zero-day exploits," "heuristic analysis," or "endpoint detection and response" with a non-technical audience can lead to confusion, disengagement, and ultimately, security lapses. Technical folks should explain complex concepts in a way that is accessible to a broader audience. Security professionals should frame security risks in terms of business impact, helping decision-makers understand the potential consequences of cyberattacks.

Security vs Convenience

Visual aids like charts, graphs, and security awareness posters can explain complex concepts in a memorable way. When we provide security awareness training for employees, we should equip them with a basic understanding of cybersecurity threats and best practices in a way that is easily understood by them.

Crossroads Dilemma

Imagine a gated community. Residents enjoy a secure environment, but access is controlled. Guests need authorization, and entry takes longer than an unrestricted neighborhood. A bank vault protects valuable assets. Accessing the vault requires additional security checks, it isn't as convenient as a Taco Bell drive-through. Onboarding an airplane requires more security checks than getting into an Uber because the stakes are higher. We all like to take shortcuts, but are we aware of the risk it invites?

Encounters in the hallway

I've been in situations in the hallway where the developer or project manager turned the other way when they saw me walk from the other side. It didn't deter me from stating my point. I think they were just kidding when they turned around and commented audibly, "Here comes the security person, let's go the other way". Before making any snap judgment, let's put ourselves in the other person's shoes for a moment. For months, the developer has been working to implement the functionalities of the application. The project manager would be held responsible if delivery deadlines are missed. Involving the security person at this stage of the project is like throwing a wrench into their plans. Security is working as a gatekeeper, pleading to hold on, not so fast. Before you move your application to production, run the security tests to confirm that your application has no security vulnerabilities.

We wrote more about this dynamic in Chapter 14, where we cover the human cost of compliance and what it feels like from both the employee's side and the auditor's side. If the hallway encounter resonated with you, that chapter will too.

Tools, Resources, and Solutions

The Ruthless Minimalism Checklist

Before buying another tool, answer these five questions honestly.

First: What problem are we solving? If you can't articulate the specific problem in one sentence, you don't need the tool yet. You need clarity.

Second: Can an existing tool solve this? Most organizations use less than half the features in their current security stack. Before adding a new product, exhaust what you already own.

Third: What are we retiring? For every tool you add, identify one to remove. If you can't find one to retire, you're adding complexity, not solving a problem.

Fourth: Who maintains this? Every tool needs an owner. If the answer is "the team" or "IT will figure it out," the tool will be misconfigured within six months and abandoned within twelve.

Fifth: What happens if this tool fails? If the failure of one product cascades into others, your architecture is too tightly coupled. Simplify the dependencies before you add more.

These five questions have saved our clients hundreds of thousands of dollars in unnecessary tool purchases. They sound obvious. That's the point. Obvious questions get skipped when the shiny toy is in front of you.

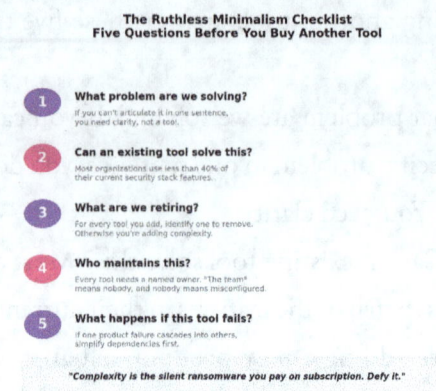

Less is more

Simplicity over Complexity

Each new tool we add to our cybersecurity arsenal comes with its own set of challenges. It requires maintenance, updates, and training. It also becomes another point of vulnerability that attackers may target. We can reduce this attack surface by prioritizing simplicity. Creating a streamlined security infrastructure requires careful thought, planning and more effort than adding layers of complexity. The payoff is a more secure and resilient organization. Before investing in new cybersecurity tools, it's essential to fully explore the capabilities of our current tools. Existing solutions offer features and functionalities that address a wide range of security needs. Organizations that embrace simplicity can build a resilient and manageable information security management system compared to an organization with a complex labyrinth of security products.

The industry is finally catching on. Three out of four organizations are actively pursuing vendor consolidation strategies. The most effective approach we've seen with our clients follows a simple three-step process: inventory, consolidate, automate. First, map every security tool in your environment and document what it does, who owns it, and what it costs. Second, identify overlaps and retire the tools that duplicate functionality. Third, automate the manual processes that remain. Our Dashr.ai platform was built on this philosophy: one view of your security posture instead of ten dashboards, automated evidence collection instead of manual screenshots, and prioritized action items instead of a firehose of alerts. Show me ten dashboards and I'll show you ten blind spots.

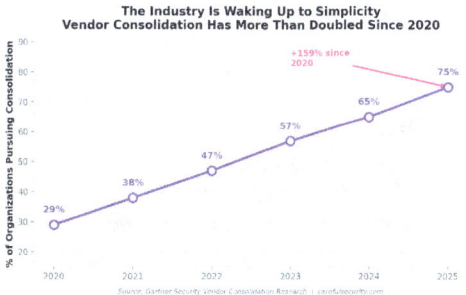

Reducing the clutter

Performance-Based Contracts

Instead of relying on demos and promises, customers could start demanding performance-based contracts with vendors. The contracts will stipulate that the vendor receives complete payment only if the product performs as promised. Hopefully, it will reward vendors to focus on delivering results instead of showcasing features. When vendors commit to being accountable, customers get more value out of their cybersecurity investments.

Open Source or Closed Source

Stability or Flexibility

Open-source or non-proprietary software allows the source code to be freely available to the public, allowing for modification and distribution. Closed source or commercial software keeps the source code private and restricted. A curious technologist may prefer open-source software because of its flexibility and customization options. Clients prefer closed-source software because of its user-friendly interfaces and vendor contracts. Some organizations provide subscription-based support for open-source software. The choice between open-source and closed-source software depends on cost, customization, support requirements, and security concerns.

Some European countries are leaning towards open-source software to remove dependency on US-based vendors. Switzerland has a new law that requires the Federal government to choose open-source software. Their belief in "public money, public code" drives them to advocate for open source software, as they believe it will enhance transparency, security, and cost-effectiveness in their government operations. The German Government is replacing the Windows platform and Microsoft Office with the Linux Platform and Libre Office. The decision was driven by their desire to promote "digital sovereignty" and protect citizens' data from foreign companies. The transition to open-source software is not only about technical advantages. It is also about supporting European tech companies and promoting European technology. They value data protection and want to reduce reliance on American corporations.

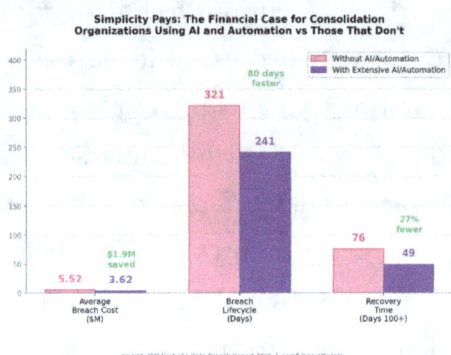

Simply Consolidate

What This Means For Your Business

The average SOC manages 45+ tools. Three out of four organizations are actively consolidating. Organizations that embrace AI and automation in security save millions per breach. The math favors simplicity. Before your next security purchase, run it through the five-question checklist in this chapter. If a tool can't survive those questions, it belongs in someone else's budget. For mid-market companies without a dedicated security team, the fastest path to simplicity is outsourcing the complexity: let a team that has done this fifty times build a streamlined security program for you, rather than assembling it piecemeal from fourteen different vendors. That's the lesson from the kitchen sink in Chapter 5 and the egg aisle at the beginning of this one. When you don't know which eggs to buy, the answer isn't more eggs. It's finding someone who knows which ones you actually need.

Chapter 7: Defense in Depth

Layers of Security

"Anything That Can Go Wrong, Will Go Wrong"

-Edsel Murphy

Murphy was an optimist. If he was working in cybersecurity, he would have most certainly liked the concept of defense in depth. If an attacker can bypass the first layer of defense, we'll intercept them at the second or third layer. Somewhat like the movie Ocean's, where the casino owners had set up multiple layers of defense to protect the casino vault.

I was chatting with a friend who also sells cyber insurance. He asked "If an employee clicks a phishing link and the entire company gets infected, whose fault is it? Should we blame the employee or the IT Security team for failing to protect the employee?" I turned the question around on him. What if someone breaks into your house while you're asleep? What would you do? He said he lived in a gated community, had locks, an alarm system, and even a gun in his bedroom as a last resort. Just like with home security, cybersecurity needs layers of protection, with different people responsible for each part.

If an employee clicks on a malicious link, there are a series of protective steps we can take to mitigate risks to the company. Did we train them about phishing? Did we have email security to catch the bad links? What about endpoint protection to stop malware? Have we limited their permissions? Are their computers up-to-date? Have we isolated their computers to prevent infection spread? The key is to have multiple layers of defense. This can stop attacks or at least minimize damage. It's not about blaming one person, but about having a sound security infrastructure in place.

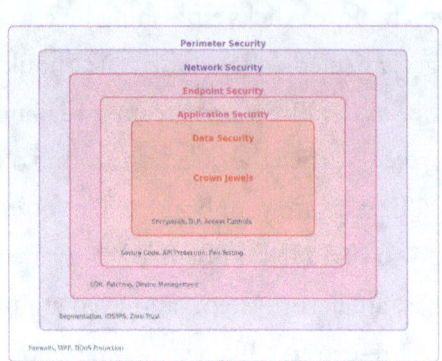

Defense in Depth

According to the IBM 2025 Cost of a Data Breach Report, more than half of breaches were caused by malicious attacks, with the remainder split between human error and IT failures. That IT failure category includes misconfigured systems, unpatched software, legacy infrastructure, and failed security tools: organizations that breached themselves without any attacker involved. The average breach took 241 days to identify and contain, the lowest in nine years, but most organizations still took more than 100 days to fully recover. Defense in depth exists precisely for these scenarios: when one layer fails, the next layer catches it.

Organizational Realities

Reactive over Proactive

Many action movies are based on the lead characters finding themselves in an unpleasant, hostile situation where things didn't go as planned and now, they must get out of it to survive. The heroic efforts and the occasional guffaws inspire us as we frantically munch the popcorn. The movie that doesn't sell is one where the hero works to improve their life routinely. A life that's so well planned doesn't counter any unexpected twists and turns. It's secure and solid, but not attractive. There's no drama! Is that the reason reactive security is more appealing than proactive security?

Neglecting Vulnerabilities

Attackers are actively scanning the internet for unpatched systems, vulnerable to known exploits. Vulnerability Management is neglected by the defenders and exploited by attackers. The repetitive process of scanning, identifying, prioritizing, and remediating security weaknesses is not exciting but worth the effort. Automated vulnerability scanning produces a standard CVSS scoring system that doesn't include the likelihood of exploitability. For example, a vulnerability on an internal workstation would have lower priority than the same vulnerability on a public-facing server. Many teams tend to defer security patches for another time when they're not busy fighting fires. Organizations with legacy software don't want to upset the apple cart. Herein comes the usefulness of creating a report that can help mobilize action.

The 2025 data makes the case even more urgently. Vulnerability exploitation as an initial access vector increased significantly from the prior year. Edge infrastructure was hit hardest: attacks on firewalls, VPN concentrators, and remote access gateways increased eightfold. Only about half of perimeter-device vulnerabilities were fully remediated, with a median fix time of 32 days. That's 32 days of open exposure on internet-facing systems that attackers are actively scanning. The Verizon 2025 DBIR put it bluntly: organizations are leaving the front door open for a month and wondering why someone walked in.

Privileged Access

System and Network administrators have access to sensitive systems. This makes them an attractive target for cybercriminals. Important accounts, like those belonging to IT, systems, and networks administrators or DevOps personnel have access to the crown jewels of an organization. Privileged accounts, especially those with weak passwords can be a prime target for attackers. Sometimes the danger comes from within. Malicious insiders or even well-meaning employees who make mistakes can cause serious damage. Privileged Access Management helps us keep an eye on who's doing what and creates a record of their activity, so that we have accountability. Without log details of privileged activities, investigation and recovery from a breach can become a nightmare.

Security by Obscurity

Security by obscurity relies on keeping security measures secretive. It's based on the belief that if attackers don't know our security systems, they can't breach them. This manifests itself in overly complex configurations, custom algorithms, or hidden resources with hard-to-find links. It assumes that attackers lack the knowledge or resources to uncover hidden information. Passwords can be cracked, URLs discovered, and complex systems can be reverse-engineered. Security by obscurity often leads to an obscure sense of security and disastrous consequences if those secrets are compromised.

The Test for Security by Obscurity

Ask yourself these questions. Is your security solution overly complex with custom rules? Does it rely on custom instructions that only you understand? Do you have hidden resources behind obscure systems and URLs? If you answered "yes" to any of these questions you may be practicing security by obscurity.

Snags in the Supply Chain

Imagine this: one single attack on a supply chain could hit hundreds, even thousands of businesses that all depend on the same supplier. It's like a domino effect. While the number of organizations directly targeted in these kinds of attacks hasn't grown too fast since 2018, the impact of those attacks has exploded.

The Verizon 2025 DBIR reported that breaches involving third parties doubled year over year, now accounting for nearly a third of all breaches. Supply chain compromise was among the most prevalent attack vectors, costing millions on average and taking the longest to resolve at 267 days. The Snowflake breach of 2024 demonstrated the pattern perfectly: over 100 companies were compromised because a cloud platform didn't require multi-factor authentication. One weak link, hundreds of victims.

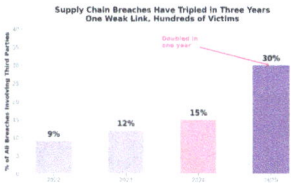

Low Hanging Fruits

Incorrect configurations, open ports, and wide-open access controls are some of the low-hanging fruits that make it easy for attackers to break in. Attackers can easily pluck low-hanging fruits such as easily guessable passwords like "password123" or default passwords for network and IoT devices without any effort. Attackers use automated tools to guess weak passwords, exploit publicly known vulnerabilities and insecurely configured web apps making unauthorized access look like a child's play.

Legacy Applications

Legacy Applications are a risk because they are no longer supported, don't have a standardized upgrade path and are dependent on tribal knowledge to keep the wheels spinning. On top of that, they often store vast amounts of sensitive data, making them attractive targets for attackers. Applications developed in-house or by third-party vendors often become part of this legacy suite, lacking proper security testing and ongoing maintenance. They turn into 'forgotten' systems that accumulate vulnerabilities, harbor outdated security practices, and lack clear ownership or support. If it's a legacy application with no upgrade path consider substitution, network segmentation and other compensating controls that can reduce the risk of a security breach.

Web Application Attacks

Externally accessible web applications are attacked by hackers because they are accessible available to anyone on the internet, and may run insecure code or configuration that attackers can exploit to gain unauthorized access. Older web applications and CMS platforms often contain vulnerabilities, such as SQL injection, cross-site scripting, or remote code execution attacks. Adversaries exploit web apps because they're easy to find, often packed with valuable customer data like credit card numbers or personal information and can provide an entryway into the users accessing the application. Applications that don't properly validate user input are susceptible to attacks where malicious code is injected into the system. Not keeping web application software and libraries updated leave them exposed to known vulnerabilities with readily available exploits.

Breaches caused by stolen or compromised credentials are one of the most common initial attack vectors. Credential misuse dominates the landscape of web application attacks. If you're a developer, you don't want to have weak passwords because web applications are externally accessible. Sometimes developers create a backdoor for troubleshooting or hard-code passwords in the code. Injection attacks pose a significant threat to API security. Attackers inject malicious code into API requests to trick the API into executing unintended commands. This can lead to data breaches, data corruption, and even complete system takeovers.

API attacks deserve special attention in 2025. As organizations adopt microservices, cloud-native architectures, and AI-powered integrations, APIs have become the connective tissue of modern applications, and a primary attack surface. The vast majority of exploited vulnerabilities in 2025 involved web applications, and stolen credentials dominated basic web application attacks. The combination of exposed APIs, weak authentication, and automated scanning tools means attackers can discover and exploit API vulnerabilities at machine speed. If your application has an API, it needs the same level of protection as your front door: rate limiting, authentication, logging, input validation, and regular penetration testing.

Tools, Resources and Solutions

Transparency and Standard Practices

Effective cybersecurity relies on transparency and adherence to established best practices. When we can confidently explain your security measures without revealing sensitive details, we're on the right track. This approach also allows for collaboration, peer review, and easier troubleshooting. We benefit from the collective knowledge and experience of the security community, making our systems more resilient to attacks.

Zero Trust Architecture

The defense-in-depth principle has a modern implementation: Zero Trust. The traditional security model assumed that everything inside the corporate network was trustworthy. Zero Trust assumes nothing is trustworthy until verified. Every user, every device, every application must prove its identity before accessing any resource, regardless of whether it's inside or outside the network perimeter. The core principles are straightforward: verify explicitly by always authenticating based on all available data, use least privilege access by limiting users to only what's needed, and assume breach by minimizing the blast radius when, not if, a breach occurs. Zero Trust isn't a product you buy. It's a strategy you implement across identity management, device security, network segmentation, application access, and data protection. For mid-market companies without the budget for a full Zero Trust transformation, start with the highest-impact controls: multi-factor authentication everywhere, network segmentation between critical systems, and least-privilege access reviews quarterly.

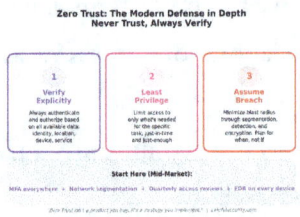

Reports that mobilize action

A vulnerability management report often ends up being numbers and percentages. If our reports look complex it gets tossed aside for another time. If we want our reports to grab the attention of the executives, we must learn the fine art of capturing the details and then hiding them from plain sight.

CISA KEV Catalog

The KEV Catalog by CISA is a collection of security vulnerabilities that have been successfully exploited and linked to ransomware campaigns.

The Verizon 2025 DBIR found that roughly half of CISA KEV vulnerabilities were fully remediated in the year they were published. That means nearly half of the vulnerabilities that are known to be actively exploited remain unpatched. The median time to remediate was 32 days. For internet-facing systems, 32 days is an eternity. Prioritize KEV catalog items above all other vulnerabilities. They are not theoretical risks. They are confirmed attack paths being exploited right now.

Vulnerability scanning reports should be complemented with a monthly patch management report to capture the progress made in remediation of the identified vulnerabilities. Patching is not always easy. It requires testing, approval, and a rollback plan.

Cyber Insurance

Cyber insurance is essential in case of a data breach. It covers the costs of data recovery and system repair. However, the insurance questionnaire can be tiresome. Sometimes, we may be tempted to answer yes to all the required controls. But this can backfire if there's a breach and the insurance company needs to verify our security measures. When purchasing a policy, it is important to carefully consider the coverage and exclusions. Does it cover scenarios like fund transfer frauds involving compromised vendors by your accounts payable team? Does it provide endorsements for regulatory coverage enhancement and intellectual property protection? Does it have reputable service providers in its panel? What is the deductible and what are the exclusions? Since most people do not understand the complexities of policy language, it is advisable to seek help from someone who does. With the rise in ransomware attacks, insurance companies were losing money to attackers. To mitigate this risk, they were advising their clients to keep insurance information confidential, as attackers were demanding the exact amount specified in the policy. Insurance companies prefer to have clients with strong security measures. It reduces the risk of a breach and allowed for lower premium payments. They like to work with third-party security providers and in-house experts to assess and reduce the risk of security breaches. It makes for a win-win partnership.

The cyber insurance market tightened significantly in 2025. Insurers are asking more detailed questions about specific controls: MFA deployment, endpoint detection coverage, backup immutability, incident response plan testing, and privileged access management. Organizations without these controls in place face higher premiums, reduced coverage, or outright denials. The IBM 2025 report found that involving law enforcement in ransomware incidents reduced breach costs by approximately $1 million, a fact that should be built into every incident response plan. Cyber insurance is not a substitute for security. It's a backstop for the risks that remain after you've done the work.

Attack Surface

Finding external exposure information falls under the realm of attack surface management. Organizations can use a combination of open-source tools and commercially available services to monitor such information. Some security companies monitor the dark web. Attack surface reports should be acted upon to lock down and reduce the attack surface. [1]

Endpoint Security

Ensure EDR software must be installed on all devices for monitoring and threat detection capabilities. Secure your

---

1. https://www.csoonline.com/article/574585/10-dark-web-monitoring-tools.html

devices by updating EDR security policies, patches and browser security settings.

Vendor Risk Assessments

Vendor risk assessments help us spot potential problems and make informed decisions. To do it right, we must review the security posture of our vendors and remediate the risks at least on an annual basis. It takes effort, but it's way better than dealing with a vendor-caused catastrophe down the road. Protecting customer data is a shared responsibility. Businesses should ensure that their partners and vendors adhere to similar strict security standards. They should establish clear contractual agreements with third parties regarding their data handling practices.

KPI Based Reporting

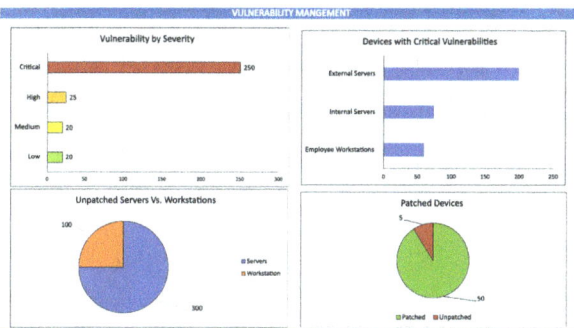

C-Suite Exec: "This report is too complex. What do you need from me?"

Cybersecurity Expert: "We have been neglecting patch management in the organization."

C-Suite Exec: "Okay, what do you need from me?"

Cybersecurity Expert: "People are not applying critical security patches. Details are in the report."

C-Suite Exec: "I can't understand the report. What do you need from me?"

Cybersecurity Expert: "Here's a visual report. Marketing is in the red."

C-Suite Exec: "I'll call up the Marketing head."

Cybersecurity Expert: "Thank you! You're awesome!"

C-Suite Exec: "So are you! "

What This Means For Your Business

Defense in depth is not about buying more tools. It's about ensuring that when one layer fails, the next layer catches the threat. The 2025 data tells us exactly where the layers are failing: unpatched vulnerabilities, supply chain compromise, stolen credentials, and human error. Start with the highest-impact layers: MFA on every publicly accessible system, endpoint detection on every device, network segmentation between critical systems, quarterly vulnerability patching prioritized by CISA KEV catalog, and vendor risk assessments for every third party with access to your data. If your C-suite executive can't read your security report in 60 seconds, redesign the report before you redesign the architecture. The dialogue at the end of this chapter isn't comedy. It's the most effective security strategy in the book: make the risk visible to the person who controls the budget.

Chapter 8: Protectors of the Castle

"Fixed fortifications are a monument to the stupidity of man."

-George S. Patton

In Los Angeles and other airports across America, the TSA has an inspiring sign on its desks and on the Wall. It says, "Not on my Watch". It's awe-inspiring and as a cybersecurity professional gives me the chills. Can we borrow the same catchline for everyone on the cybersecurity team? The cybersecurity team is like TSA folks guarding the airport. They inspect people's luggage; we inspect network traffic. They validate identities at different checkpoints, we ensure there is a strong authentication and authorization processes. Security is only as strong as its weakest link, and even a seemingly minor oversight, like leaving a backdoor open for convenience, can be exploited by attackers. Analysis of major security breaches often leads to the simplest of mistakes. Someone forgot to deactivate a dormant account, someone left a remote connection service listening on the public network, someone forgot to enable multi-factor authentication on a privileged account, etc.

The IBM 2025 Cost of a Data Breach Report found that human error and IT failures contribute to almost half of all breaches. Cybersecurity professionals face constant pressure to stay ahead of evolving threats, which is leading to a burnout crisis. The ISC2 2025 Cybersecurity Workforce Study surveyed a record 16,029 professionals and found alarming levels of exhaustion across the field.

Nearly half of cybersecurity professionals feel exhausted from trying to stay current on the latest threats and emerging technologies. Almost as many feel overwhelmed by workload. Job satisfaction has declined for three consecutive years. Layoffs, budget cuts, hiring freezes, and promotion freezes have compounded the problem, with the largest organizations hit hardest across all four measures. Only about a third of respondents said they have the right level of cybersecurity staffing. We have a field that is simultaneously understaffed and burning out the people it does have. The castle's protectors are exhausted, and the walls are getting thinner.

The Cybersecurity Blues

You run around disheveled, trying to convince your superiors of all the vulnerabilities that need to be fixed but no one seems to care until one day when they do. But it's too late by then. Your worst fears have come true. The intruder is inside the house. The next three weeks fly by in a haze. Poring through the evidence, retracing the attack path, speculating what happened, and responding to management on the extent of the damage. You didn't realize that one of those days was your birthday or a vacation planned with the family. While one team is working on isolating and neutralizing the attack the other team is rebuilding systems from scratch. All this could have been avoided. You have been talking about these risks for the last six months. If only they listened to you. Cybersecurity is not a field for the faint of heart. It demands a high tolerance for pain. There are no easy answers or one-size-fits-all solutions. Success requires a willingness to confront difficult situations head-on.

Organizational Realities

Mr. Robot : Hollywood vs Real Life

Mr. Robot: Hollywood vs Real Life

The Emmy-winning show Mr. Robot tracks the life of Elliot Anderson, who works as a cyber-security engineer by day and a vigilante hacker by night. The show's characters are highly intelligent people who use a variety of hacking techniques to gain access to computer systems. It doesn't take them a long time to break into organizations. In one of the scenes, Elliot claims that in 3 short minutes, he destroyed a man's life, business, and existence. Day-to-day cybersecurity at corporate jobs is often less glamorous, involving processes, ticket creation, and documentation. A team of intelligent individuals doesn't always translate to robust security. Most cybersecurity professionals I know have a short attention span and little or no penchant for processes and paperwork. So, what do they do? They turn their attention to cool research projects and the newest technological innovations that'll do the job for them. This focus on novelty can stem from intellectual curiosity, a desire to escape monotony, and aspirations for recognition and career advancement.

The Blue Team

The Blue Team is made up of people working in the Security Operations Center. They form the first line of defense against cyberattacks. The blue team can sometimes turn blue staring at a blue screen, blasted with a barrage of security alerts most of which are false positives. False positives are generated from benign user activities and not actual security alerts. Closing security alert tickets is like playing a game of whack-a-mole. Sometimes blue teamers get graded on the number of tickets they close in a day. That should not be the case: prioritize quality over quantity.

AI is reshaping the Blue Team's work in ways that create both relief and new anxiety. Most organizations are either already using AI security tools or planning to implement them. Professionals broadly view AI as a positive development, seeing it as handling time-consuming and repetitive tasks rather than replacing the human element. The good news is real. Organizations using AI and automation extensively saved $1.9 million per breach and cut detection time significantly. But the flip side is real too. AI is now the number one skills gap, and analysts who can't work alongside AI tools risk falling behind. The Blue Team of 2025 doesn't just close tickets. They manage AI systems, validate AI-generated alerts, and make judgment calls that machines can't. The role got harder, not easier.

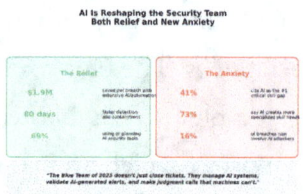

Security Analyst

As a new cybersecurity analyst, I felt excited during the interview process with a big organization. I thought my life would change forever if I got to join this team of successful and intelligent people. However, once inside, it was "Déjà Vu all over again". The infrastructure of the new organization appeared just as porous as my last rodeo. I realized that the view from the outside rarely matches the view from the inside. Inside the shiny hallways of every corporate organization are worried cyber security analysts carrying with them the knowledge of unpatched servers and insecure web applications.

Practice what we preach

In cybersecurity, the concept of "eating your own dog food" suggests that security professionals and privileged IT users adhere to the same security standards they recommend to the rest of the organization. This often isn't the case. Security professionals, despite having access to the most sensitive systems and creating the rules, may not always follow these rules themselves. This phenomenon isn't unique to cybersecurity. Professionals across various fields often fail to practice what they preach. Doctors might neglect the health advice and dietary restrictions they prescribe to their patients, financial advisors might not follow their own investment strategies, web designers might have outdated personal websites, etc. This inconsistency between words and actions erodes trust and credibility.

When security teams prioritize their own security, not only do they protect themselves they also inspire others to take security seriously. System and network administrators have access to sensitive systems, making them attractive targets for cyber-criminals. Important accounts, such as those belonging to IT, systems, and network administrators, or DevOps personnel can provide crucial information within an organization. Accounts with weak passwords are especially vulnerable to attacks. The threat can also come from within, with malicious insiders or well-meaning employees who make mistakes causing significant damage. Privileged Access Management helps monitor and track user activity, ensuring accountability. Without detailed logs of privileged activities, investigating and recovering from a breach can become a nightmare.

Just this once

I never speed just this once

The problem with the 'just this once' shortcut is that we get habituated to it and forget to reverse the change. For example, if I change this firewall rule, I can manage it from my home network without having to login to the company VPN. We open it, test it, it doesn't work, we try something else and then something else and forget to close all the 'just this once' accesses. The firewall gets compromised a few months later. Imagine you're someone who always drives within the limit but breaks it just this one time because you're in a rush and you get pulled over for it. Will the police officer let you off the hook because it was just one time?

The developers may have left a break fix backdoor that gets discovered and exploited months later. An employee received an urgent email from a client containing sensitive customer information. He forwards the email to his personal account so he can work on it over the weekend. His personal email gets hacked, compromising the client data and putting his corporation at risk of regulatory fines. When someone gets away with a "just this once," bypass, it creates a precedent for others to do the same and erodes the overall security culture. How can we effectively manage these "just one time" situations? Document it in a ticket, request for approval and exceptions, and then track it to make sure the change is reverted as soon as feasible.

Can someone tell me what my job is?

There can be a lack of clarity in cybersecurity job roles and responsibilities. Job descriptions are poorly defined and often combine multiple roles into one position. They also use technical jargon that can be disconnected from the actual tasks. The new nature of cybersecurity positions leads to a lack of standardization in titles and terminology. Job descriptions often have unrealistic expectations for proficiency in programming languages, operating systems, and tools. To address these issues, clear requirements for roles should be promoted, including job qualities and skills. Hiring should be more flexible, focusing on capabilities over certifications. Frameworks like the NICE Framework can be used to define work roles, competencies, and tasks.

The Smartest One in The Room[1]

Many cybersecurity teams boast of highly intelligent and capable individuals, but this doesn't always translate to robust security. The "best and brightest" may prioritize

---

1. The Smartest Person in the Room: The Root Cause and New Solution for Cybersecurity: Christian Espinoza

learning new technologies and pursuing innovative projects and neglect the mundane yet essential. The focus on novelty can stem from a desire for recognition, career advancement, and the allure of higher positions. Nothing is wrong, but someone must do the basics. As talented individuals rise through the ranks, they gain greater influence and control over resources. This can lead to a detachment from the day-to-day operations. The focus shifts towards strategic initiatives and vendor relationships, leaving the fundamental security tasks to others who may lack the same level of expertise.

The Adversarial Advantage

Attackers are often driven by financial gain or other malicious intent. They have a laser focus on achieving their goals, even if it means investing significant time and resources. In contrast, security teams face competing priorities and resource constraints, making it challenging to maintain the same level of focus and urgency. In some cases, attackers may be more skilled or resourceful than the defenders. The constant cat-and-mouse game of cybersecurity means attackers are evolving their tactics, making it difficult for the security teams to stay ahead. While new technologies are important the fundamentals of cybersecurity cannot be ignored. Simple, repeatable tasks like patching vulnerabilities, monitoring logs, and educating users are essential for maintaining a strong defense. When these tasks are seen as mundane and less rewarding it can lead to negligence and errors. Understanding the human dynamics helps us develop effective strategies for building and maintain a strong security posture.

Shifting Priorities

In cybersecurity, work doesn't always follow the plan you made at the beginning of the day, week or month. You start work with a set schedule in mind. I am going to configure these firewalls, create some new deny rules, forward logs to the monitoring system and observe the anomalous traffic in the network. Unfortunately, a new critical vulnerability just got discovered, it doesn't have a security patch, and it's all over the news how hackers are exploiting this vulnerability. Now you must scan all your systems to find how the new vulnerability affects your organization. If it does, you must shift priorities and put controls in place before the adversary can exploit it. Just another day in a security professional's life. To survive the constantly changing landscape we must be nimble and ready to adapt.

Living inside the cave

Security professionals like to live inside their dimly lit dark cave to run their practices. They do not like to meet people or speak with people IRL. Yes, that is a term coded by the people living with keyboards. Cybersecurity professionals can't afford to be isolated. Sitting in an office and meticulously crafting attack models alone won't stop attackers. We must get out of our comfort zone, engage with the people and systems we're protecting, and collaborate on addressing risks. Security professionals should work with other departments, such as IT, Software Developers, Human Resources, Legal departments, and executives, to create a comprehensive security posture. They need to communicate technical concepts to non-technical audiences to gain buy-in for security initiatives. Inside the security echo chamber only agreeing opinions are heard and different viewpoints are ignored. Software developers with vulnerabilities in their code are often criticized. The IT team does not care about security's opinion. Management views security as an obstacle. Everyone understands each other's frustrations and collectively express sighs of disappointment. Everyone sympathizes with each other and sighs a collective sigh.

The shift to remote and hybrid work has permanently expanded the castle's perimeter. The Verizon 2025 DBIR found that nearly half of compromised systems were unmanaged devices: personal laptops and phones outside IT's control that stored both personal and corporate credentials. Attacks on VPN concentrators and remote access gateways increased eightfold. The castle no longer has defined walls. Its protectors must defend a distributed workforce accessing sensitive systems from home networks, coffee shops, and airports. This makes endpoint detection, zero trust architecture, and identity management more critical than ever. You can't protect what you can't see, and in a hybrid world, the security team sees far less than it used to.

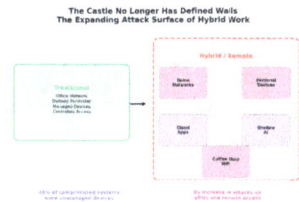

Insider Threats

A disgruntled former programmer, with access to the source code and disgruntled by a recent layoff, stole valuable intellectual property and sold it to a competitor. The breach went unnoticed for months.

Compared to other attack vectors, malicious insider attacks resulted in the highest costs, averaging $4.92 million per breach according to the IBM 2025 report. What makes insiders so expensive is dwell time: insider breaches take longer to detect because the activity looks legitimate. The credentials are real. The access is authorized. The behavior only becomes suspicious in retrospect.

What could we have done differently? Data Loss Prevention Tools could have been utilized to block sensitive data from leaving the network. User activity logs could have been reviewed to alert against unusual file access patterns, data exfiltration attempts, or privilege escalation activities. Access rights could have been restricted, and segregation of duties put in place to protect the crown jewels. Continuous monitoring along with well-coordinated incident response processes would have alerted for insider threats, minimized the potential impact and preserved critical assets.

Competing with the Deadline

Security professionals face a dilemma. Other departments want their changes implemented as soon as possible and we must ensure that it doesn't create any new vulnerabilities. Sometimes we have the backing of the supervisors, sometimes we don't. It's a delicate balance that demands courage and conviction. A security breach can have significant consequences for the company. As a cybersecurity professional, our true employer isn't the charismatic VP pushing for the latest flashy tool, or a friendly colleague seeking a temporary exception in the firewall restrictions. Our allegiance lies with the organization and its stakeholders. Don't let the allure of short-term gains or political pressures sway our decisions. Have the courage to say 'no' when necessary, and the conviction to prioritize safety over convenience. Remember, we're not a roadblock, we're the bridge to a safer future.

Human Vulnerabilities

Over-Sharing

Over-sharing access to files and folders is like handing over an entire mountain when all you need is a single plant. This not only makes it harder to find the information you need but also exposes unnecessary data to potential risks. In the realm of cybersecurity, less is often more. By carefully controlling access and adhering to the principle of least privilege, we can significantly reduce your organization's risk exposure. Over-sharing can be particularly dangerous when dealing with sensitive data. For example, when collecting information from employees, focus on capturing only what is necessary. Avoid collecting and storing excessive personal details that could be exploited if a breach were to occur.

Security as an afterthought

Imagine constructing a magnificent house, only to realize halfway through that forgot about the plumbing. That's the reality many companies face when they retrofit application security as an afterthought. Companies often prioritize speed over security, leading to costly retrofitting down the line. Integrating security throughout development is like building a secure house from the start.

Failing to communicate risks

The Chief Information Security Officer struggles with limited resources. She may have a clear vision but lack the backing of the board. When she reports to the board on the progress made and roadblocks faced, the report contains the metrics, jargon, and justifications that the board doesn't understand. To build trust with the board, the CISOs must understand the business operations first. When the CISO is not a regular at board meetings, it can lead to a lack of trust and communication. When the CISO reports to the CIO or the CTO who may prioritize other technology initiatives instead of investing in security there could be a potential conflict of interest.

The SEC's enforcement actions following the SolarWinds breach changed the stakes for CISO communication. CISOs and executives can now be held personally accountable for material cybersecurity misrepresentations. This means the board report isn't just an internal document. It's a legal record. The metrics need to be accurate, the risks need to be stated plainly, and the resource gaps need to be documented. If the board says no to a security investment and a breach occurs in exactly the area that was flagged, the documentation protects both the CISO and the organization. The C-suite dialogue in Chapter 7 captures the communication challenge perfectly: if the executive can't understand the report, it's the report's fault, not the executive's. KPIs beat OMGs. Boards fund numbers, not adjectives.

Working in Silos

Teams work independently because of various factors, such as conflicting priorities, disagreements between managers, and a lack of overall coordination. As a result, the approach to security becomes fragmented, with each team focusing solely on their own goals rather than considering the organization's overall security posture. Security breaches rarely arise from a single point of failure; they usually result from a breakdown in multiple areas within the system. The absence of a comprehensive security strategy leads to a tendency to prioritize individual projects in isolation.

Tools, Resources and Solutions

Challenging the Status Quo

Cybersecurity threats are constantly evolving. Relying solely on security measures that worked in the past may not work in the present.Cybersecurity, like anything else in life, is a practice of continuous challenge and continuous improvement. We should not be accepting the "We've always done it this way" answer.

Cybersecurity: "Your file server is accessible to everyone in the network."

IT: "That's because one of the folders needs to be accessible to everyone."

Cybersecurity : "Who's accessing it? Can we separate the shared access from the restricted access?

IT: "Nobody knows. We can try to restrict and hope nothing breaks."

Cybersecurity: "Can we also enable user audit logging, so that we can track the traffic?

IT: "We can do it, but if anyone screams we'll blame you"

Heads I win tails you Lose

Security professionals are lightheartedly called troublemakers but spare a thought for them. They will get blamed in the event of a security compromise. Security should step up their game by providing guidance and hands-on assistance to reach the desired outcome. If we can make the change look simpler by breaking it down into manageable steps, we empower our employees and build allies within the organization. At the same, those responsible for security should feel empowered to reject questionable requests and unfulfilled requirements. It is challenging to say "No" when people are passionate about their ideas and plans. Rejections from security can be deterring. We should be open to addressing the other teams concerns.

The Ethical Hacker

Penetration testing plays a crucial role in manually identifying vulnerabilities in systems and processes. It's important to note that each new test can uncover previously unknown weaknesses, so it's unfair to expect a penetration tester to find all vulnerabilities in the initial test. Attack patterns and exploitation tactics evolve alongside vulnerabilities, which is why it's worth considering using a different tester to gain a fresh perspective. While testers may showcase impressive techniques for circumvention, attackers are typically looking for the easiest path to exploit. It is commonly believed that given enough time and resources, almost anything can be hacked, unless it's a well-hidden secret buried deep in the desert sand. It is crucial to define the scope of testing and know when to stop.

Security as a Business Enabler

A few years ago, I received a high five from a Senior Vice President at a large corporation. She came to us for a solution to a problem that she thought would violate the company's security policy. The issue was that she needed to automatically route support tickets to the vendor, but e-mail forwarding was not allowed due to privacy concerns. We made sure to thoroughly check the support tickets for any sensitive information. Our recommendation was for her to use a shared mailbox and create a guest account for the vendor to access the support tickets. This solution allowed her business to function smoothly without going through the typical security review process.

This experience was memorable because it showed me the impact we can have as a "solution provider" instead of a "pain provider." We transformed our image from being a "blocker" to an "enabler." Rather than simply saying "no," security experts should strive to find win-win solutions and support the organization's objectives. It's important to remember that cybersecurity is not meant to hinder progress, but to enable it with necessary safeguards. When we position ourselves as problem solvers with viable solutions, we change the perception of security from being a roadblock to being a supporter of the organization. This approach builds trust, encourages cooperation, and makes security measures more accessible.

A bipartisan view

Instead of living inside an echo chamber where our perspective is limited and does not reflect the full picture, let's challenge ourselves to have a bi-partisan view and consider both sides of the solution. When everyone agrees with the powerful and the loud people in the room, we become dismissive of fresh new ideas. No one wants to speak up or rock the boat. But that's precisely where we can challenge ourselves to innovate with a bi-partisan view.

The Value of Unstructured Exploration

Allowing time for unstructured exploration can foster creativity and innovation. Google's famous twenty percent time policy, where engineers have one day a week to pursue their passion projects, led to breakthroughs. Giving cybersecurity professionals freedom to pursue their own interests can yield unexpected benefits. However, it's important to find a balance between exploration and job responsibilities. Rabbit holes can be interesting, but they can also lead to a loss of focus and productivity. Cybersecurity professionals must be mindful of how much time they spend on specific issues, especially when there are urgent tasks. It's easy to feel overwhelmed by the amount of information and potential threats. To avoid getting lost, professionals should prioritize their work and set boundaries. They should allocate time for exploration without neglecting their primary responsibilities. It's important to remember that there is always more to learn, but the goal is to protect the organization and its assets. By finding the right balance between exploration and action, professionals can grow personally and ensure organizational security.

Sharing Intelligence

Intelligence flows seamlessly between teams in a circular model. The blue team shares defense observations with the risk management team. They assess the risks and vulnerabilities. The red team then validates these findings. They attempt to exploit the vulnerabilities and provide concrete evidence for attack scenarios.

Karate Kid

If you're a passionate cybersecurity analyst, don't let yourself become "that angry kid." Constantly complaining about risks isn't going to win you any friends. Instead, focus on building relationships with people from other teams. When you spot a risk, don't just talk about it – write it down clearly and present it to your manager along with possible solutions and how much effort they might take. This shows initiative and makes it way easier for your manager to escalate. Remember that not everyone speaks tech. Tailor your communication to your audience, explaining complex stuff in simple terms. Your goal is to help people understand and fix security risks, not to show off your knowledge. Make yourself indispensable. Go the extra mile, always exceed expectations, and document your achievements to show your boss how valuable you are. Cybersecurity is like martial arts – we need to be flexible, adaptable, and always ready to try new approaches.

Executive Blessing

Once the problem and solution has been clearly defined, it's time to get the executives' approval. It is a necessity for any cybersecurity project to succeed. The SolarWinds attack was a wake-up call. The SEC (Securities and Exchange Commission) is now holding companies and their executives accountable for cybersecurity failures. It's serious business now, and everyone needs to be on board. The CISO (Chief Information Security Officer) should be able to demonstrate how security efforts help the company achieve its goals. When talking to the higher-ups, it's about explaining security in terms of business risk. Following the rules and avoiding security breaches builds customer trust, which is good for business. Security can save money by streamlining things, getting rid of old systems, and making the company less vulnerable to attacks. When security starts talking the same language as the executives, they're more likely to support security initiatives. The CISO should report directly to the CEO or CFO and stay independent so they aren't influenced by other departments. The CEO and CFO can help ensure that the security strategy aligns with the company's overall goals.

Collaboration over Conflicts

Security Leadership should recognize and acknowledge expertise of leaders from other departments. Collaboration is the key to avoiding conflicts. When we understand C-Suite's concerns and goals, we can tailor our message to address their specific needs. Identify the individuals who have a vested interest in cybersecurity within the organization. Enlist them in discussions about risks, solutions, and exceptions. When encountering resistance, emphasize the business impact of cybersecurity risks. Instead of blaming, teams should work together to take responsibility. It starts with strong leadership from a CISO who champions security initiatives and fosters a security-conscious culture, communicates risks, vulnerabilities, and cybersecurity dos and don'ts across all levels of the organization.

What This Means For Your Business

Your security team is exhausted. Nearly half feel burned out, and job satisfaction has dropped steadily for three years. Budget cuts and hiring freezes have made the problem worse, not better. If you're a mid-market company, you likely don't have a dedicated security team at all, which means your IT team is carrying the security load on top of everything else. The practical options: invest in your people through training, certifications, reasonable workloads, and recognition. Augment with external expertise for specialized functions like penetration testing, compliance, and incident response. Implement AI-powered security tools that handle the repetitive work so your humans can focus on the judgment calls that matter. The high-five story in this chapter isn't just a feel-good moment. It's the model. When security becomes an enabler instead of a blocker, everything changes: the culture, the cooperation, and the outcomes. Protect the protectors, and they'll protect the castle.

Chapter 9: Social Engineering Attacks

This is your President speaking

"Only amateurs attack machines; professionals target people."

-Bruce Schneier

In September 2023, MGM Resorts International, a major casino and hotel chain in Las Vegas experienced a ransomware attack. The attack disrupted the functioning of slot machines, hotel key cards and online reservations used by guests. MGM lost over 100 million dollars to an attack that was started by a social engineering attack. The attackers used "vishing" or 'voice phishing' to impersonate an IT supervisor who called IT because they were locked out of their account. Once the attackers gained access to the supervisor's account, they exploited other security vulnerabilities in the infrastructure to launch a ransomware attack.

The messaging app, Twilio fell victim to a data breach when a social engineering attack was launched on one of their employees. The attacker stole the employee's credentials, gained access to internal systems, and exfiltrated customer data. An accidental click on the wrong email can be costly. Millions of dollars are lost in business downtime, investigation, and damage control activities.

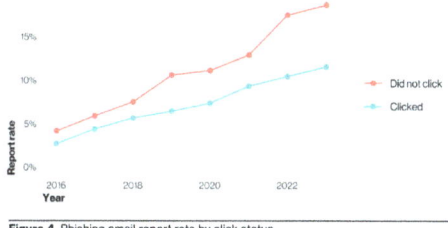

Figure 4. Phishing email report rate by click status

According to Verizon Data Breach Report 2024, 20% of users fell for phishing traps during simulation engagements. Only 11% of the users who clicked on the link reported to IT about it. The median time for users to click on a malicious link after opening the email is 21 seconds. It took another 28 seconds for users to enter their data on the phishing link. The median time for users to fall for phishing traps was less than 60 seconds. We wanted to test the report numbers for ourselves. After discussing with the client, we sent out a phishing email from a non-corporate account, pretending to be a nearby Bobba shop. Our story was that we partnered with corporate HR to reward employees who pay attention to their emails and respond promptly. The first 30 people to respond to this email with their drink of choice will get a free Bobba. The rush of responses came in within the first 30 minutes before employees verified with HR and realized something's not right. Some people responded and later recalled the email but by then we already had their name, email and favorite Bobba drink.

Organizational Realities

Usual Targets in Social Engineering attacks

C-Suite Leadership, HR and Finance team have access to confidential company assets. The HR and Client service team often interact with external parties. They receive links and suspicious attachments more than others. IT administrators are also a common target for adversaries as they have elevated access to the IT infrastructure.

Pre-texting

Attackers have become increasingly sophisticated, moving away from immediate "kill" tactics to slower, more deliberate approaches. They build rapport with their targets over time, creating a sense of trust and familiarity. This makes victims more likely to comply with requests, such as opening a seemingly harmless attachment that could contain malware.

Figure 34. Top Action varieties in Social Engineering incidents (n=3,647)

Too many Phish in the Sea: Spear Phishes

Attackers research their targets in advance through social media or additional publicly available information to craft a personalized phishing email that is likely to trick their target. They may pose as a representative from a reputable organization or even a colleague, manager, or executive within the target organization. Once the attacker gathers enough information about their target, they craft an email that appears legitimate and trustworthy. The email is designed to look as authentic as possible, often replicating the style, tone, and signature of the impersonated individual or organization. The email will usually include a request or some urgency for encouraging the target to act quickly, which might involve clicking a link, downloading an attachment or providing sensitive information.

Business Email Compromise: BEC

Business email compromise (BEC) attacks can be highly effective. The U.S. Federal Bureau of Investigation calls BEC the "$43 billion (about $130 per person in the US) scam," referring to statistics for incidents reported to the Internet Crime Complaint Center. In a BEC attack, actors use spear phishing tactics to carry out fraudulent activities. They compromise an employee's email account and send messages from the employee's account to request fund transfers or other sensitive information. BEC attacks can take several forms, such as CEO fraud where attackers provide misleading instructions from a Senior Executive's account. The median transaction for a BEC related compromise is around $50,000. When you realize you are a victim of BEC promptly report it to law enforcement. In half of the cases, law enforcement was able to recoup the losses, however in 18% of the incidents the victims lost everything that was sent to the criminals.

BEC vs Phishing

In a BEC attack, the email address used is legitimate. In phishing attacks, the email account belongs to the threat actor or is fraudulent. To initiate a BEC attack a threat actor may use phishing tactics to steal credentials and gain access to legitimate business email accounts.

Brand Impersonation

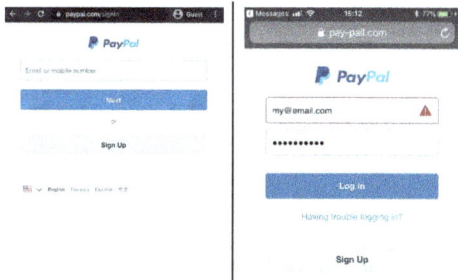

Which one is real?

Brand impersonation is a type of spear phishing attack where the attacker impersonates a well-known brand or organization to trick the target into providing sensitive information. Brand impersonation attacks often involve creating a fake website or email that appears to be from a legitimate source, using logos, branding, and other details to make the attack appear authentic. Brand impersonation attacks can take several forms, such as creating fake login pages that look authentic or sending a phishing email that appears to be from a legitimate brand.

Credential Harvesting

Threat actors trick users into divulging login credentials to gain access to their online accounts or sensitive information by posing as a reputable organization or service. In a credential harvesting attack, the attacker usually sends a fake email or creates a fake website that appears to be from a legitimate organization such as a bank or social media platform. Then, he or she asks the user to provide their login credentials.

During Hillary Clinton's 2016 presidential campaign, the chairman for the campaign, John Podesta became the victim of a spear phishing attack. The attack began when the chairman received an email, which appeared to be from Google, asking him to change his email password. The email contained a link directing him to a fake Google login page, which prompted him to enter his credentials. The attacker used the stolen credentials to access Podesta's email account and the email accounts of other campaign staffers. The attackers then downloaded and exfiltrated thousands of emails and documents, which were later leaked to the public.

Clone Phishing

In a clone phishing attack, the attacker typically starts by obtaining a legitimate email sent to the target in the past, such as a marketing or promotional email from a trusted brand. The attacker then creates a near-identical copy of the email, often using the same branding and layout but with a few key differences. For example, the attacker may change the sender's email address, the links in the email, or the attachments, to make the email appear more urgent or legitimate.

Payment Frauds

Attackers may also compromise a vendor or supplier's email account to request payments or send incorrect financial information. Payment fraud scams usually target the accounts payable team. The email would contain a request to change the vendor's banking information. The employee may follow the instructions, believing it to be legitimate. However, the email would have been sent by cybercriminals who gained access to the vendor's email account and posed as the vendor. The attackers use this access to send fraudulent payment requests, which when approved and processed may result in the loss of millions of dollars.

Tools, Resources, and Solutions

Multi-factor Authentication

Having multi-factor authentication increases the security on your email account. Multi-factor authentication means there are two checks in place to prove your identity before you can access your account. For example, you may need to supply an authentication code from an app as well as your password. It makes it more difficult for someone to access your files or account. Use a strong passphrase for your email account if you cannot use multi-factor authentication.

Email Security Configurations

Implement DMARC (Domain-based Message Authentication, Reporting and Conformance) to mitigate the risk of email spoofing. Use SPF (Sender Policy Framework) and DKIM (DomainKeys Identified Mail) to further authenticate emails and prevent spoofing. Consider AI-powered email protection tools that analyze email content, sender behavior, and other factors to detect and block suspicious emails.

Social Engineering Tests

We have to be proactive to fight back against social engineering attacks. Running tests that mimic real-world traps, like fake emails or phone calls, can reveal weak spots in employee awareness. Plus, these tests can help you create training programs that are spot-on, addressing those specific areas where your team might be vulnerable.

User Awareness

Educating your employees is crucial. They are often the first to encounter attacks, so they need to know how to recognize and respond to them. Training should cover common tactics like phishing and pretexting. Employees should feel comfortable reporting any suspicious activity, no matter how small. Taking these extra steps can make a big difference. Proactive testing and training can help identify and fix vulnerabilities before they are exploited. Well-trained employees are less likely to fall for tricks, reducing the risk of a successful attack. Even if an attack occurs, educated employees are more likely to catch and report it quickly, limiting the damage. Social engineering attacks are constantly evolving, so continuous training and testing are essential to stay ahead. Inform them about free online tools like virustotal.com to check the legitimacy of suspicious links. At the same. Remind them that "curiosity killed the cat".

Chapter 10: The Boy who cried Wolf

"If you fail to plan, you are planning to fail"
-Benjamin Franklin

The story of "The Boy Who Cried Wolf" teaches a valuable lesson about the importance of honesty and the dangers of lying. A young shepherd boy gets bored while watching his sheep and decides to play a prank on the villagers. He shouts "Wolf! Wolf!" causing the villagers to rush to his aid, only to find no wolf. He finds this amusing and repeats the prank again fooling the villagers. When a real wolf appears and the boy cries for help, no one believes him. The boy learns a lesson that if you lie too often, people will stop believing you, even when you're telling the truth.

Don't be a Target

The Target Security breach in 2013 was a classic example of the consequences of missing security alerts. The attackers got in by leveraging a third-party vendor's login details and installing malware on Target's point-of-sale systems. Even though the SIEM system noticed something strange, the alert was ignored due to alert fatigue and the absence of proper incident response protocols. As a result, millions of customers had their credit and debit card information stolen.

As outlined in the IBM Data Breach Report, Security Incident and Event Management (SIEM) and Incident Response (IR) planning are two of the top factors in reducing the cost of a breach.[1] SIEM monitors our infrastructure against security anomalies and Incident Response planning documents the detailed actions to be taken in the event of a security incident.

---

1. https://www.ibm.com/reports/data-breach

Factors that reduce average breach cost

Organizational Realities

Finding the Scapegoat

The average time to detect a breach is 6-9 months. By the time an intrusion is discovered the intruders may have wiped off their footprints. When a breach is found, the security team must take responsibility. They cannot blame the leadership, their peers or their supervisors. Let's say you identified some legacy applications with low hanging fruits waiting to be plucked by unauthorized intruders. When you raised it to the departmental head, they didn't want to make tough decisions on fixing the old server issues. They lightheartedly blamed you for creating more work when there's already plenty to go around. Now that there's an actual incident and you are asked for an explanation, do you say, I already told you about this issue three months back. Security analysts may find themselves to be living in a world of professional paranoia.

The hunt for a scapegoat begins once a security incident is under control. Assigning blame rarely leads to meaningful results. It's more of a mad scramble to escape the axe through corporate finger-pointing.

SOC (Blue Team): "The monitoring system was too noisy we missed the real alert."

Ethical Hacker (Red Team): "We never tested the new system you went live too early."

CISO: We're working on new automation technology. But we haven't implemented it yet.

GRC (Compliance Team): "If you followed the company security policies, the breach could have been prevented"

Cybersecurity Vendor: "We sent you the new tool, but it wasn't configured yet."

Regulatory Bodies: "You must pay the penalties; personal data got disclosed."

Cyber Insurance: "We can't make the full payment you didn't look at the alerts"

SIEMs easy but not really

The lack of clear objectives can impede the rollout of the SIEM. Without well-defined goals and use cases, organizations struggle to determine what they want to achieve with their SIEM. SIEMS may not capture the important security event logs or end up capturing unnecessary logs. Log management tools help organizations manage the high volume of log data generated across the enterprise. They can assist in determining what data and information needs to be logged, the format in which it should be logged, the duration for which the log data should be saved and how data should be disposed of or destroyed when no longer needed.

SIEM solutions are complex. They require continuous fine-tuning, rule updates and system upgrades to keep up with emerging threats. Integrating a SIEM with existing security tools and infrastructure can be a challenge. Compatibility issues, data format inconsistencies, and lack of vendor support can hinder successful integration, limiting the effectiveness of the SIEM. Without proper filtering and correlation, this leads to alert fatigue and an overwhelming number of false positives, making it challenging to identify real threats.

Setting up and managing them requires skilled personnel to configure, tune, and monitor the system. Failure to allocate resources for ongoing maintenance leads to performance degradation and security gaps. Inadequate training and awareness among employees is another factor that undermines the effectiveness of a SIEM. Even with a well-implemented SIEM, employees need to be trained on how to use and interpret the data. Organizations that cannot address these factors end up with a SIEM that generates more noise than actionable insights, hindering their ability to detect and respond to security threats.

Weakness in Incident Response process

Organizations often fail to implement a working Incident Response (IR) process for several key reasons. One reason is underestimating the importance of IR. Some organizations view IR as a reactive measure rather than a critical component of their overall security strategy. This mindset can lead to inadequate resource allocation and a lack of commitment to establishing an effective IR process. A robust IR process requires meticulous planning, including defining roles, responsibilities, and communication channels. Failure to invest time in upfront planning can lead to confusion and delays during an actual incident.

Miscommunication or lack of communication can hinder incident response efforts, causing confusion, delays, and potential escalation of the issue. Even with a well-defined IR process, employees need to be trained in their specific roles and responsibilities during an incident. Without proper training, individuals may not know how to respond appropriately leading to ineffective incident handling. A successful IR process requires regular testing and refinement through tabletop exercises and simulations. If organizations don't test their incident response process, they won't know about weaknesses until it's too late. Effective IR often relies on specialized tools and technologies for incident detection, analysis, and response. Organizations with limited budgets or outdated infrastructure may struggle to implement such a process due to resource constraints.

Alert Fatigue

The Target Security breach in 2013 was a classic example of the consequences of missing security alerts. The attackers got in by leveraging a third-party vendor's login details and installing malware on Target's point-of-sale systems. Even though the SIEM system noticed something strange, the alert was ignored due to alert fatigue and the absence of proper incident response protocols. As a result, millions of customers had their credit and debit card information stolen.

Alert fatigue is a significant concern, especially for blue teams working long shifts. After hours of chasing down false positives, it's easy to become complacent and dismiss alerts without thorough investigation. This can have disastrous consequences if a real threat slips through the cracks due to an analyst's exhaustion or eagerness to clear their workload. The key to addressing alert fatigue is improving the accuracy of alerting systems. Fine tune the monitoring system to reduce false positives and prioritize true threats. By investing time and effort in refining these processes, organizations can save resources and ensure that security analysts can focus their attention on real threats rather than chasing phantom alarms. Regular maintenance and adaptation of alerting systems to the evolving threat landscape are crucial to maintaining a strong security posture.

Tool, Resources, and Solutions

Organizations that fail to plan for incident response or lack clear recovery procedures may have to negotiate payments with cybercriminals. It is important to have secure backups and a tested plan for fail over and disaster recovery in case of a security breach. To improve security monitoring process lets start by defining your security monitoring goals and metrics.

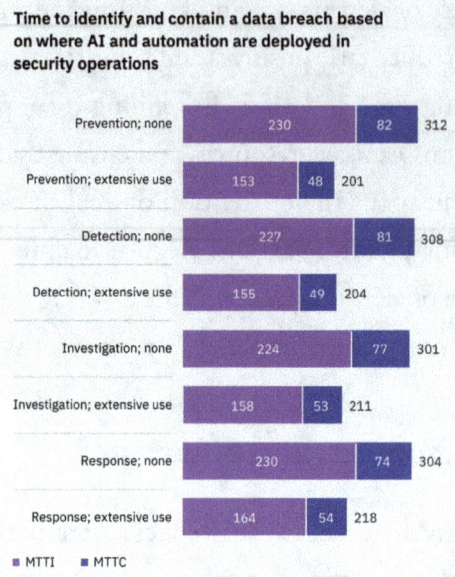

Organizations that extensively use security AI and automation can identify and contain data breaches much faster. On average, they do so nearly 100 days (about 3 and a half months) faster than organizations that don't use these technologies at all.

Tuning the SIEM

SIEM (Security Information and Event Management) systems are essential tools in the cybersecurity landscape. They are like a CCTV monitoring system that provides visibility into inbound and outbound traffic. To enrich the SIEM, we need to feed it security logs aka camera feeds from all the relevant sources. The SIEM uses these feeds to create a timeline of activities. The timeline would show the entry and exit points of malicious activities. However, SIEMs cannot track every bit of user and network traffic. Instead, they focus on identifying unusual or abnormal activity. For example, a user suddenly logging in from an unexpected location would trigger an alert. SIEMs need time and training to understand normal traffic patterns within an organization. This "tuning" process is crucial to minimize false positives and ensure that alerts are relevant and actionable. As an organization's network traffic evolves, so must the rules and parameters of the SIEM. Organizations with limited resources can enhance their monitoring capabilities with automated threat detection and response.

Business Impact Analysis (BIA)

When an organization conducts a Business Impact Analysis (BIA), it can determine the potential impact of various systems on business operations. Without an official exercise, this knowledge gets lost. Understanding the criticality of different systems allows security teams to prioritize high-impact systems. A BIA is often the first step in developing an incident response plan. A BIA assists in the incident response process by identifying critical functions, prioritizing recovery efforts, developing response plans, communicating risk, estimating downtime, and prioritizing security investments.

Chapter 11: The Impact of AI

Let me AI that for you

"It's going to be interesting to see how society deals with artificial intelligence, but it will definitely be cool."

-Colin Angle, Co-Founder of iRobot

When computers were first introduced to the workplace, people of my father's generation panicked. They were these new, fancy, and expensive machines, and nobody really knew how they'd be used. People were scared that computers would basically take over all the jobs and leave everyone unemployed. It's similar to when

ATMs first showed up. People were worried they'd put bank tellers out of business. ATMs actually made banking more convenient and even led to new customer service jobs. Can you imagine waiting for the bank to open to withdraw some cash? What is cash by the way, you may ask.

Hollywood and AI

Living in Los Angeles I have some friends in the entertainment industry. We're having a fun chat at a local brewery when the conversation naturally turned to Hollywood's fear of being replaced by AI. A lot of the artists that I know created masterful scripts or performances based on some of the most struggling days of their life. Creative work as I understand is based on pain, loneliness and being down and out and then rising back like a Phoenix. Did AI ever get depressed thinking about its challenging childhood growing up with an absentee mother or an alcoholic father? No it didn't. It cannot replicate the human emotions, trials and tribulations. An algorithm cannot replace a human, but can it reduce the drudgery of parsing through log files looking for an attacker's footprints? Can it identify security anomalies without feeling fatigue at the end of a long 8-hour shift?

The IBM 2025 Cost of a Data Breach Report confirms the financial case for AI in security. Organizations using AI and automation extensively saved $1.9 million per breach and reduced their breach lifecycle by 80 days. The global average breach cost dropped to $4.44 million, the first decline in five years, driven largely by AI-powered detection and containment. But most organizations are not yet using AI extensively in security operations. The majority are leaving millions on the table.

The Dark side of AI

AI and automation have both positive and negative effects on cybersecurity. Cybercriminals are using AI to create sneaky malware, send convincing phishing emails, and exploit system vulnerabilities more quickly. They are using AI to generate polymorphic malware that is harder to detect and analyze. Attackers are using AI tools to develop malicious products and solve problems related to processing user data dumps. It has lowered the entry barrier for criminals, enabling rookies to perform attacks that previously required experienced teams. In terms of cyber defense, AI still has a long way to go. While it will have a significant impact on security in the future, new technologies often benefit attackers before defenders.

The numbers confirm what security teams feared. A growing share of breaches now involve attackers using AI, with AI-generated phishing and deepfake impersonation leading the categories. Shadow AI, where employees use unsanctioned AI tools, became a measurable factor in breaches, adding significant extra costs per incident. Most breached organizations lacked AI governance policies entirely. Nearly all that experienced AI-related security incidents had no AI access controls. And for the first time, IBM tracked breaches directly impacting AI models or applications themselves. AI is both the best defense and the newest attack surface. Chapter 15 covers the governance frameworks, including ISO 42001, that organizations need to manage this dual reality.

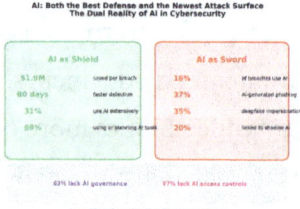

AI-Based Social Engineering Attacks

Cyber criminals are using artificial intelligence tools for phishing and social engineering attacks, as well as voice and video cloning scams. AI enhances attackers' capabilities and boosts the speed, scale, and automation of cyber-attacks. Cybercriminals are using AI tools, both publicly available and custom-made, to launch highly targeted phishing campaigns. They are creating convincing messages with proper grammar and spelling, increasing the chances of successfully deceiving and stealing data. AI-powered voice and video cloning techniques are being used to impersonate trusted individuals, family members, co-workers, or business partners. Generative AI is increasingly being used to create sophisticated phishing attacks, enabling even non-native English speakers to craft grammatically correct and convincing messages.

Privacy and security concerns

AI is a bit of a black box sometimes. It can make decisions and predictions, but it's not always clear how it got there. This lack of transparency can be a bit unsettling, especially when it comes to sensitive information. Plus, AI systems are often trained on massive amounts of data, which raises concerns about who has access to that data and how it's being used. It's like trusting a stranger with your diary: you want to be sure they're not going to spill your secrets.

AI Rules and Regulations

The rules around AI are no longer the Wild West. The EU AI Act is now the most comprehensive AI legislation in the world, with prohibited AI practices banned since February 2025 and high-risk AI enforcement taking effect August 2026. ISO/IEC 42001, published in December 2023, provides the first certifiable standard for AI Management Systems. The NIST AI Risk Management Framework offers voluntary governance guidance in the U.S. South Korea enacted its AI Framework Act effective January 2026. Japan passed its AI Basic Act in May 2025. The patchwork is becoming a quilt, and organizations that aren't preparing now will find themselves scrambling when enforcement catches up to their AI deployments. We cover this in depth in Chapter 15.

Concerns around 'job security'

It's like that scene in Terminator where the machines rise and take over. But AI is more likely to change the way we work, not completely replace us. Sure, some tasks might become automated, but that also opens opportunities for new roles and skills. It's about adapting and learning to work alongside AI, not fearing it.

Tools, Resources and Solutions

NIST AI Framework

The NIST RMF Playbook offers detailed, voluntary guidance to organizations on how to implement the AI Risk Management Framework (AI RMF). It aims to help organizations enhance their ability to design, develop, use, and evaluate AI products, services, and systems in a trustworthy manner. The Playbook is structured around the four core functions of the AI RMF: Govern, Map, Measure, and Manage, and provides specific suggestions, transparency and documentation tips, and resources for each subcategory within these functions. It emphasizes a multidisciplinary and multi stakeholder approach to AI risk management, recognizing the complex interplay of technical, societal, and ethical considerations in AI development and deployment. By following the Playbook's recommendations, organizations can proactively address AI risks, foster trust, and ensure the responsible and beneficial use of AI technologies.

How cybersecurity teams can use AI

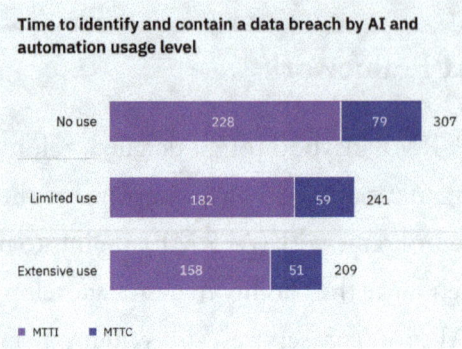

AI in cybersecurity can be super-smart assistant that's always on the lookout for trouble. It can spot those sneaky new threats within network traffic, user actions, or system logs, stuff that might slip past us mere mortals. If we can catch the bad guys we can reduce the damage. AI can also be used to find security vulnerabilities, it can scan our assets, highlight the critical findings and associated security patches. AI can also be a master at spotting anomalies, whether it's on the network, an individual device, or even in how users log in. It can help detect phishing emails and fake messages. We're talking about security systems that can crunch massive amounts of data to spot unusual patterns and potential threats in real-time. We can also create automation rules to isolate infected computers, block bad traffic, and send out alerts. By catching breaches early, we can stop them quickly and prevent data loss. The need of the hour is skilled cybersecurity folks who know how to use the AI-powered tools effectively.

AI Adoption Process

Before adopting any AI tool, it's essential to conduct a thorough review to ensure it aligns with your organization's security and privacy requirements. Start by evaluating the vendor's reputation and track record. Scrutinize the tool's data handling practices, including how data is collected, stored, and protected. Assess the transparency of the AI algorithms and whether they can be audited or explained. Consider the potential for bias and ensure the tool has been tested for fairness. Finally, have a clear understanding of the tool's capabilities and limitations, and ensure it integrates seamlessly with your existing security infrastructure.

What This Means For Your Business

AI is not optional. Organizations using AI extensively in security save $1.9 million per breach. Those that don't are leaving that money on the table while facing attackers who are using AI against them. The practical steps: deploy AI-powered email security and endpoint detection, the highest-impact applications. Establish an AI governance policy before your employee creates shadow AI liabilities. Conduct an AI inventory to know what AI tools are operating in your environment. And start evaluating ISO 42001 if you deploy AI in products or services. The organizations that govern AI responsibly will use it as a competitive weapon. The ones that don't will find it used as a weapon against them.

Chapter 12: Ransomware Attacks

Ostritch in the Sand

Hoping for the best, prepared for the worst,
and unsurprised by anything in between.
                                    -Maya Angelou

The Optimism Bias

During COVID, some people believed they were in good health and had never had any health problems before, so they thought they had high immunity and wouldn't catch COVID. Young people, especially, felt invincible, like they always do, but they still got sick. "Optimism Bias," leads us to believe that bad things can happen to others but not to us. There was a sense of complacency and rebelliousness which led to people not taking the necessary precautions. Unfortunately some of them ended up getting the virus and regretted not taking the precautions. This is similar to not preparing for the "ransomware attack" as readily available preventive measures can significantly reduce the risk of an incident. Just as masks and vaccines helped protect people from contracting and spreading COVID-19, proper cybersecurity practices like data backups, employee training, and updated software can prevent or mitigate the damage caused by ransomware attacks. If we refuse to consider the severity of an adverse impact, we are more likely to neglect the precautions.

According to the Verizon 2025 Data Breach Investigations Report, ransomware now appears in nearly half of all reviewed breaches, nearly doubling from the prior year. But the nature of ransomware is changing. Attackers increasingly skip the encryption entirely and simply steal the data, threatening to release it publicly unless payment is made. The ITRC's 2025 Annual Data Breach Report confirmed that ransomware incidents decreased as attackers shifted to pure data theft and extortion. The business model evolved, but the threat didn't shrink. It just changed shape.

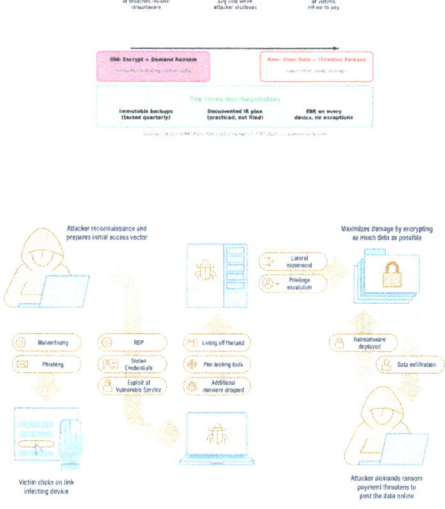

Figure 1 - High-Level Overview of a Typical Ransomware Attack.

Overview of a ransomware attack

The WannaCry ransomware attack targeted the security vulnerability in the SMB file-sharing protocol used by Microsoft Windows computers. The attack caused an estimated $4 billion in damages globally and spread to over 150 countries. Once a computer was infected the malware self-propagated autonomously without any user interaction to other vulnerable computers on the same network. Microsoft was aware of this security vulnerability and released the patch in March of 2017. Organizations had two months to patch the security vulnerability as the attack was launched in May 2017. The attack emphasized the risks posed by outdated systems and served as a wake-up call for many organizations that didn't conduct prompt and proactive patching.

The Marks & Spencer breach in April 2025 demonstrated how ransomware continues to evolve. The Scattered Spider group used phishing to trick IT staff at a third-party vendor into resetting admin credentials. The resulting ransomware attack disrupted e-commerce operations across more than 1,400 M&S stores, caused an estimated 300 million pounds in lost revenue, and wiped approximately 1 billion pounds off the company's market value. The initial access vector wasn't a sophisticated exploit. It was a phone call.

The economics of ransomware shifted in 2025. On-chain payment tracking by Chainalysis recorded roughly $820 million in ransomware payments. Most ransomware victims now refuse to pay. But refusing doesn't eliminate the cost. The average expense of a ransomware or extortion incident reached $5.08 million when disclosed by the attacker. Organizations with tested incident response plans and immutable backups were the ones that could refuse. Organizations without them were the ones writing checks. The IBM 2025 report found that involving law enforcement reduced ransomware breach costs by approximately $1 million, a stat that should be built into every incident response plan.

Organizational Realities

Partial Coverage

In cybersecurity, there's a big difference between 99% and 100%. Attackers try to get into our networks by exploiting weaknesses in our public-facing applications and remotely accessible services. A lot of these attacks are successful because of basic security oversights. Things like not having multi-factor authentication for that one account used for third-party remote access can become a way to get in. Misconfigured permissions or outdated software are also major culprits. Other vulnerabilities include weak passwords, open ports and misconfigured services that managed to slip through the cracks. Also, endpoint detection and response aren't up to par, attackers can use sneaky scripts and PowerShell attacks to bypass your defenses.

Partial Backups

Regular and secure data backups are essential in preventing data loss due to ransomware. When ransomware encrypts files, the most effective way to recover data without paying a ransom is to restore from a recent, clean backup. Keeping backups offline or in a secure, cloud-based solution protects them from being accessed or encrypted by ransomware. These backups should be immutable so that nothing can modify or delete them. It is also critical to frequently test recovery processes to ensure that data can be restored quickly and effectively. By maintaining an up-to-date backup system, organizations can minimize downtime, reduce the financial impact of an attack, and avoid paying ransoms.

Partial EDR

EDR (Endpoint Detection and Response) tools are highly effective against ransomware. These tools use advanced techniques like behavioral analysis and machine learning to identify ransomware attacks before they cause significant harm. EDR solutions can automatically isolate infected devices, stop the encryption process, and even roll back affected files to their original state, minimizing damage. By offering visibility into endpoints and providing proactive defense mechanisms, EDR tools greatly enhance an organization's ability to prevent, detect, and respond to ransomware attacks.

What are the primary challenges your organization faces in implementing technology solutions for ransomware defense?

(Select all that apply)

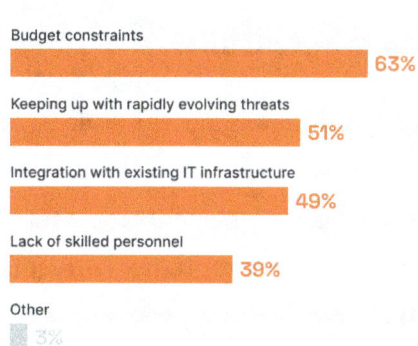

Challenges in implementing Ransomware Defense

Tools, Resources and Solutions

#StopRansomware Guide

CISA's stop ransomware guide[1] provides guidance for organizations to best practices to prepare for, prevent, and mitigate ransomware incidents and data extortion attacks. It starts with the importance of regular backups. Make sure you've got them, they're immutable, and they're stored offline or in an air gapped network . Next up, have a plan in the event of a cyber incident response plan. Make sure everyone knows what to do and who to call if ransomware strikes. Keep your systems and software up to date with the latest patches for e.g. SMB, and be careful about what services you expose to the internet. If you need remote access, make sure it's locked down tight with strong passwords and multi-factor authentication. Train your people to spot those phishing emails and suspicious links. Use email filters and security tools to block it before it hits the inbox. Monitor for any unusual activity that could signal an attack is brewing. If the worst happens

---

1. https://www.cisa.gov/stopransomware/ransomware-guide

and you do get hit with ransomware, don't panic. Isolate the infected systems, report the incident to the authorities, and start your recovery process. Remember, paying the ransom doesn't guarantee you'll get your data back, and it might even make you a bigger target in the future.

Ransomware Defense

The Blue Print for Ransomware Defense[2] highlights the importance of keeping a close eye on all your devices, software, and user accounts. We need to know what you're protecting. Strong passwords and multi-factor authentication help secure access to these information assets. If we can take care of the basics such as firewalls, anti-malware software, and use good old-fashioned common sense we can keep your house clean and tidy and make it harder for unwanted guests to sneak in.

---

2. https://securityandtechnology.org/wp-content/uploads/2022/08/IST-Blueprint-for-Ransomware-Defense.pdf

Tabletop Exercises

Regularly conduct tabletop exercises to test and refine the incident response plan and ensure everyone understands their roles and responsibilities. Establish clear communication protocols for internal and external stakeholders during an incident. Consult with legal and public relations teams to ensure compliance with regulations and manage public perception during and after an attack.

Backups and Recovery

Establish a reliable backup and recovery strategy with frequent backups, offsite storage, and regular testing to ensure data can be restored in case of an attack. Immutable and current backups can be a game changer in ransomware attacks, allowing organizations to restore their data without paying a ransom. Recovering from a cyberattack should also include reviewing and rebuilding systems and processes and collaborating with key stakeholders from the rest of the organization. Organizations can mitigate the risk of ransomware attacks through a multi-faceted approach that combines technical safeguards, employee education, and robust incident response planning.

What This Means for Your Business

Ransomware appears in nearly half of all breaches. The average cost when disclosed by the attacker is $5.08 million. Most victims now refuse to pay, but only if they have the backups and plans to recover without paying. The three non-negotiable defenses: immutable backups tested quarterly, not just configured but tested. A documented and practiced incident response plan with defined roles and communication channels. And endpoint detection deployed on every device without exception. If your backup strategy has never been tested with an actual restore, you don't have a backup strategy. You have a hope strategy. And hope is not a plan for ransomware.

Chapter 13: Risky Business

"80% of output is produced by 20% of input."

-Pareto's Principle

Risk management is a discipline that encompasses finance, insurance, occupational safety, environmental protection, law, public health and information security. You can take all the necessary precautions and yet be surprised by a visit from our friendly neighborhood hackers. Like health insurance that offsets the cost of an unexpected health incident, we assess and mitigate the risks from potential cybersecurity incidents.

Enter "Honey-To-do list": the list that never forgets. How could you if it's stuck right in front of you on the refrigerator.

Damage from Cybercrime

According to Statista Market Insights, the global cost of cybercrime reached $10.29 trillion in 2025 and is projected to climb to $13.82 trillion by 2028. If we haven't fallen victim until now, it doesn't mean our run of luck will continue forever.

Organizational Realities

Risk assessment questionnaires

We sometimes receive a 400-question risk assessment questionnaire from a company, and we have to answer every question. It's painstaking and time consuming, but necessary. However, I doubt the effectiveness of a spreadsheet-based questionnaire that will be analyzed by software and presented to management for regulatory compliance. I'd prefer to have a conversation with a doctor to find out what exactly is wrong with my blood sugar levels rather than making assumptions from a generic blood test. Risk assessments are like a trip to the doctor. The results need context. Why are these numbers high? What does it mean? Can we get to the root cause? Yet risk questionnaires are managed by answering only the mandatory questions and striking through the rest? What I have is for you to find out. You're the doctor!

I find conversation with people more valuable. When they share some tidbits, and one thing leads to another and before you know we've opened a can of worms.

The 2025 data support the conversational approach. Organizations with comprehensive risk assessment processes and tested incident response plans saved $1.49 million per breach. But the risk assessment must be real. Auditors in ISO 27001 certifications consistently flag superficial risk assessments as one of the top findings. Generic risk scenarios copied from templates, likelihood and impact ratings that are identical across every row, treatment plans that say "mitigate" without specifying how, when, or who. A risk register that reads like a to-do list is useful. A risk register that reads like a template is liability documentation. Chapter 14 and Chapter 16 both address how to build risk assessments that auditors respect and that actually reduce risk.

The Risk Register

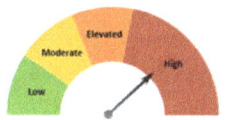

With a myriad of potential cybersecurity initiatives, determining where to start or what to address first is a significant challenge. Risk assessment is a structured approach that helps prioritize cybersecurity risks based on their potential impact and likelihood. This enables organizations to allocate resources more effectively. By identifying and addressing the most critical risks, organizations can focus on the most impactful areas, making the best use of limited resources. A risk register is a prioritized list of identified risks, including relevant details such as their descriptions, impact levels, and statuses. Many auditors gauge the maturity of a cybersecurity program by looking at the risk register to see how organizations identify, document, prioritize, and manage the risks.

Establish a risk review cadence. Annual risk assessments are the minimum compliance standard. Quarterly reviews with stakeholders ensure the register stays current and relevant. Every time there's a significant change, a new system deployment, a vendor change, an acquisition, or a regulatory update, reassess the affected risks. A risk register that was last updated twelve months ago is a historical artifact, not a management tool.

We cannot see our own eyelashes

Let's face it, there are things about ourselves that we just can't see. Just like we can't see our own eyelashes without a mirror, organizations often have blind spots when it comes to their security posture. They may be too close to their own operations to spot vulnerabilities or biases. Having a third-party assessment can provide a fresh set of eyes and help uncover those hidden risks.

Cost-Benefit Analysis

When deciding whether to invest in a security measure, it's crucial to weigh the potential costs against the expected benefits. This means looking at the likelihood and impact of a threat, how much the security measure would cost to implement and maintain, and the potential losses it could prevent.

Security Exceptions

Security exceptions may happen in almost every organization. In the hustle and bustle of our daily work, it's easy to bypass security controls. It's like taking a shortcut through a dark alley, it might save you time but it puts you at risk. Unmonitored exceptions are like ticking time bombs. They can accumulate over time, creating a vast array of security risks. To manage these risks, organizations need a formal process for requesting, approving, and tracking security exceptions. This process should include regular reviews to ensure that exceptions are still necessary and that the risks are being properly managed.

Tools, Resources and Solutions

NIST Cybersecurity Framework

Think of the CSF as a cybersecurity GPS. It offers a set of guidelines and best practices for organizations to manage their cybersecurity risks. It's like a roadmap that helps you identify, protect, detect, respond, and recover from cyber threats. Consider it your cybersecurity destination. The list below shows the complete map you choose your own path.

NIST CSF 2.0, released in February 2024, added a sixth core function: Govern. This addition reflects the growing recognition that cybersecurity governance, including risk management strategy, organizational context, and supply chain risk, must sit alongside the original five functions: Identify, Protect, Detect, Respond, and Recover. For organizations pursuing ISO 27001 or SOC 2, the CSF 2.0 Govern function maps naturally to the management system requirements that auditors evaluate.

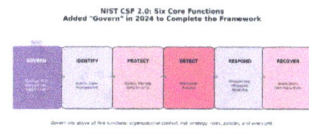

NIST Frameworks empower organizations to take a more proactive, risk-based approach to managing cybersecurity. NIST and CIS can be complementary tools for improving our organization's security posture.

Compensating Controls

Compensating controls offer a practical way to address vulnerabilities when ideal solutions are not feasible. These controls act as additional safeguards, providing an alternative means of protection in situations where primary security measures might be lacking. They can be temporary solutions while a more permanent fix is being developed or implemented. Compensating controls can bridge the gap between what is recommended and what is achievable, given the constraints of cost, technology, or operational requirements. Examples of compensating controls include network segmentation, enhanced monitoring and logging, access restrictions, encryption, and manual processes that complement automated systems.

Internal IT vs External Security

Internal IT teams play a vital role in supporting day-to-day operations and keeping the lights on. However, their recommendation for user awareness, patch management, and vulnerability scanning may not carry the weight it needs to mobilize action. Senior management may not take notice because they think the IT team is just trying to justify their budget or add more work to a busy schedule. When a third-party cybersecurity firm comes in and delivers the exact same findings, we've found that senior management may be more open to accepting it. We are not making this up, our clients themselves have shared this with us.

MSPs vs MSSPs

Doctors Vs. Specialists

An MSP is your general IT doctor. They handle the everyday stuff: setting up your computers, managing your software, and keeping your network running smoothly. They are IT solution providers with support contracts. An MSSP is a specialist. They focus specifically on cybersecurity, providing security monitoring, threat detection, incident response, and security program management. While MSPs may offer some basic security services, MSSPs bring a deeper level of expertise. Think of it like needing surgery: you wouldn't go to your general practitioner, you'd want a specialist. It's not about replacing your MSP. It's about adding specialized security expertise on top of your existing IT support. It's like having a regular doctor for general checkups and a specialist for more complex issues. As the old adage goes "A tool is only as good as the person using it".

An MSP is your general IT doctor. They handle the everyday stuff: setting up your computers, managing your software, and keeping your network running smoothly. They are IT solution providers with support contracts. An MSSP is a specialist. They focus specifically on cybersecurity, providing security monitoring, threat detection, incident response, and security program management. While MSPs may offer some basic security services, MSSPs bring a deeper level of expertise. Think of it like needing surgery: you wouldn't go to your general practitioner, you'd want a specialist. It's not about replacing your MSP. It's about adding specialized security expertise on top of your existing IT support. It's like having a regular doctor for general checkups and a specialist for more complex issues. As the old adage goes "A tool is only as good as the person using it".

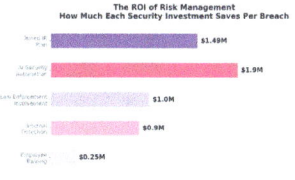

What This Means for Your Business

Risk management isn't exciting. It doesn't make headlines and it doesn't win awards. But organizations with tested risk processes save $1.49 million per breach. The practical steps: build a risk register and keep it updated. Every risk needs an owner, a timeline, and a treatment plan. Conduct risk assessments through conversation, not just questionnaires. Review exceptions quarterly and close the ones that have expired. Present risk to the board in business terms: revenue impact, insurance costs, deal velocity. Not technical jargon. And consider a third-party assessment, because as this chapter says, we cannot see our own eyelashes. The insider-outsider dynamic isn't a weakness. It's the reason external assessments consistently find gaps that internal teams have been staring at for years.

Chapter 14: The Hammer of Compliance

The Insider-Outsider Dynamic

"The best way to find out if you can trust somebody is to trust them."

— Ernest Hemingway

We've been providing cybersecurity consulting and compliance services to our clients for a while now. Through these years of practice, we've learned a thing or two about people and politics. When we step into a new organization, we're outsiders looking in. We see things the insiders can't. Like visiting a friend's house for the first time, you notice the creaky stairs, the leaky faucet, and the weird smell coming from the basement. Your friend is so used to it they don't notice anymore. That's us when we walk into a new engagement.

We find the security gaps that internal teams have been staring at for so long they've become invisible. Sometimes it's a misconfigured firewall rule, sometimes it's an entire server farm running end-of-life software. The insider-outsider dynamic is real. Internal teams may resent the outsider's findings, especially when they've been flagging the same issues for months. The outsider's report carries more weight with leadership because it's independent, objective, and comes with the authority of someone who has done this fifty times before.

The regulatory landscape isn't getting simpler. SOC 2 has become table stakes for B2B SaaS companies. ISO 27001 is the international standard that opens doors to European and enterprise markets. HIPAA remains non-negotiable for healthcare. PCI DSS governs anyone touching payment card data. And now ISO 42001 adds AI governance to the mix. The organizations that treat compliance as a strategic investment rather than a regulatory burden are the ones closing enterprise deals, reducing insurance premiums, and passing due diligence with flying colors.

The IBM 2025 Cost of a Data Breach Report found that organizations with a high level of noncompliance with regulations faced an average breach cost of $5.05 million.

Security is Compliance but Compliance is not Security

A study by the Ponemon Institute revealed that many organizations encountered a data breach despite following the basic regulatory compliance measures. How could that happen? Compliance alone isn't enough to protect against all cybersecurity threats. While compliance frameworks are essential, they often represent a baseline or minimum standard. Compliance checklists can't capture every possible attack vector. Attackers are innovative, and compliance standards may lag behind their latest tactics and techniques. Security is a marathon of continuous improvement. The compliance gap reminds us that achieving compliance is just the beginning.

The Human Cost of Compliance

We spend a lot of time talking about frameworks, controls, and auditor expectations. We don't spend nearly enough time talking about what compliance feels like for the people living through it.

Engineers hired to build product find themselves spending 20 to 30 percent of their time collecting evidence, documenting processes, and answering auditor questions. IT teams already stretched thin keeping the lights on are told to add compliance to their workload with no additional headcount, no additional budget, and no reduction in their existing responsibilities. The compliance initiative lands on whoever is closest to the problem, not whoever has the capacity or expertise to handle it.

Then comes control fatigue. The team just finished a grueling SOC 2 Type 2 marathon, and now someone announces they need ISO 27001 as well. When organizations manage these frameworks in silos instead of mapping the 80% overlap, employees end up doing duplicate work for what feels like the same thing twice. Wasted effort is demoralizing. Repeated wasted effort is a resignation letter.

The documentation burden generates its own special brand of frustration. Technical teams will tell you, sometimes loudly, that they're already doing the security work. They're running access reviews, patching systems, monitoring alerts. But because nobody documented it in a format the auditor accepts, it doesn't count. "If it isn't documented, it didn't happen" feels punitive to people who've been doing the work all along.

Policies that exist on paper but don't reflect how the organization actually operates make the problem worse. Generic template policies downloaded from the internet often bear no resemblance to the daily workflow. Employees are asked to attest to processes they've never followed.

Perhaps the most demoralizing grievance is what happens after the audit. Teams work intensely for months, pass the audit, get the certificate, and watch the organization immediately revert to its old habits. Compliance becomes an annual performance rather than a way of operating. Employees who invested real effort feel their work was disposable. The certificate goes on the website, the controls go on the shelf, and nothing changes until next year's audit cycle starts the scramble again.

A Note From the Other Side of the Table

We've talked about what compliance feels like for the people inside the organization. Now let's talk about what it looks like from the auditor's chair. Because if you want to pass your audit on the first attempt, understanding what frustrates auditors is just as valuable as understanding what frustrates your team.

"They called us before they were ready." This is the number one auditor frustration. Organizations under timeline pressure schedule the audit before their controls are actually implemented and operating. One auditor put it this way: you don't schedule the home inspection before the house is built.

"The evidence doesn't match the policies." Organizations write beautiful policies. Quarterly access reviews. Formal change management approvals. Documented incident escalation chains. Then the auditor asks for proof, and there's nothing. Auditors call this paper compliance, and they spot it within the first hour.

"The risk assessment is a template, not an analysis." Auditors can tell immediately when a risk assessment was downloaded from the internet and filled in without thought. Risk assessment is the engine of ISO 27001. When it's superficial, the auditor knows the entire management system may be performative.

"Management review is a formality." When the management review minutes show a 15-minute meeting with no decisions, no action items, and no follow-up, it signals that compliance is something the organization endures rather than something leadership drives.

"They fixed the symptom, not the root cause." Organizations that close findings with "we fixed it" without investigating the underlying cause are almost guaranteed to see the same finding next year.

Point in Time Evaluation

An audit is a point-in-time evaluation. We don't want an audit to be a dress rehearsal. We want it to be a confirmation of what we're already doing right. The best audits are anticlimactic because the organization has been operating its security program consistently, not scrambling to prepare in the weeks before the auditor arrives.

Tool, Resources, and Solutions

Compliance is aimed at the common good of ensuring a consistently secure environment. Like speed limits placed on the road, when we deviate there are consequences. The challenge is making compliance feel less like a speed trap and more like guardrails that keep everyone safe.

If it isn't documented, it didn't happen. This is the golden rule of compliance. Auditors can't verify what isn't written down. The documentation doesn't need to be elaborate. It needs to be accurate, consistent, and retrievable.

PCI vs HIPAA

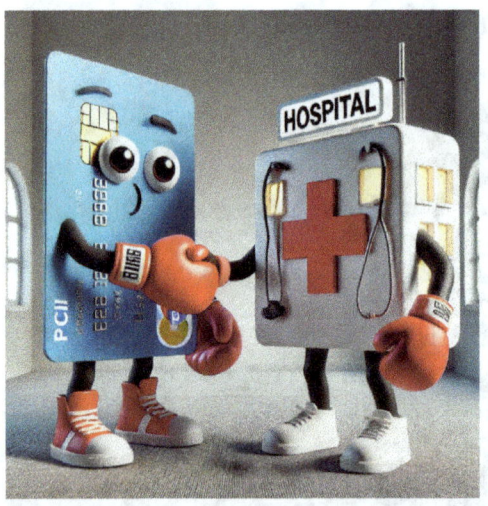

PCI controls were created to protect cardholder data during payment card transactions. Organizations try to limit their PCI scope, environment and the number of systems that handle, process, and store cardholder data. HIPAA protects the privacy and security of individual health information. The overlap between PCI and

HIPAA is meaningful for healthcare organizations that also process payments: both require access controls, encryption, audit logging, and incident response procedures.

What This Means for Your Business

Compliance isn't a tax. It's the price of doing business at scale. Organizations with high noncompliance face $5.05 million average breach costs. Every major enterprise customer, insurance underwriter, and investor ask for compliance certification. The human cost of doing it wrong, burned-out engineers, adversarial audits, annual compliance scrambles, is entirely preventable with the right approach. Chapter 15 covers the newest compliance frontier: AI governance. Chapter 16 shows you the 90-day methodology that eliminates the pain described in this chapter.

The New Sheriff in Town

Chapter 15: The New Sheriff in Town

> *"We always overestimate the change that will occur in the next two years and underestimate the change that will occur in the next ten."*
>
> — Bill Gates

The Seatbelt Moment

Remember when seatbelts were optional? Cars existed for decades before anyone thought to regulate how safe they needed to be. People drove fast, got hurt, and the industry shrugged. It took Ralph Nader's "Unsafe at Any Speed" in 1965 and years of public pressure before seatbelt laws became standard. The technology existed long before the governance caught up.

We're living through the same moment with artificial intelligence.

Companies have been deploying AI for years. Some knowingly, some without realizing that the chatbot on their website, the algorithm screening resumes, or the fraud detection engine processing credit card transactions all qualify as AI systems under emerging regulations. The technology has outpaced the rules. But the rules are catching up. Fast.

In December 2023, the International Organization for Standardization published ISO/IEC 42001, the world's first certifiable standard for Artificial Intelligence Management Systems. Think of it as ISO 27001 for AI. Where ISO 27001 provides a framework for managing information security risks, ISO 42001 provides a framework for managing the risks that come with developing, deploying, and using AI systems. Bias. Transparency. Accountability. Data governance. Human oversight. The things that can go wrong when algorithms make decisions that affect people's lives, careers, and finances.

Going back to our seatbelt analogy: you can install them before the law requires it, or you can wait until after the accident. The organizations that move early will be the ones closing enterprise deals while their competitors are still figuring out what ISO 42001 even stands for.

Organizational Realities

Let's start with the regulatory landscape, because it's moving faster than most boardrooms realize.

The EU AI Act is now the most comprehensive AI legislation in the world, and its enforcement timeline is already underway. Prohibited AI practices were banned in February 2025. General-purpose AI model obligations kicked in August 2025. The majority of remaining rules, including requirements for high-risk AI systems, take effect in August 2026. Enforcement powers and fines follow on the same timeline: up to 35 million euros or 7% of global annual turnover, whichever is higher. By August 2027, even AI systems that were already on the market before the Act need to be compliant. OpenAI has already been fined 15 million euros by Italy's Data Protection Authority for training models on personal data without a clear legal basis.

"That's Europe," you might say. "We're based in the U.S." True. But if you sell to European customers, process data from European users, or have European partners in your supply chain, the EU AI Act applies to you. And the pattern we saw with GDPR is instructive: Europe regulates first, then the rest of the world follows. South Korea enacted its AI Framework Act effective January 2026. Japan passed its first AI-specific Basic Act in May 2025. In the U.S., the NIST AI Risk Management Framework is gaining traction as a voluntary governance standard and state-level AI legislation is accelerating. The window between "optional" and "required" is closing.

But regulation is only half the story. The bigger problem is what organizations are doing to themselves.

The FOMO-driven deployment. 87% of AI projects never make it to production. Gartner projects that over 40% of ambitious agentic AI projects will be canceled by 2027 due to escalating costs and unclear business value. Companies rush into AI because their competitors are doing it, not because they've defined a specific business problem AI should solve. PwC observed that instead of leadership setting strategy with a top-down program, many companies take a ground-up approach, crowdsourcing AI initiatives they then try to shape into something like a strategy. The result: projects that may not match enterprise priorities, are rarely executed with precision, and almost never lead to transformation. McKinsey confirms 88% of organizations use AI in at least one function, but fewer than 40% have scaled beyond pilot. That's not an adoption problem. That's a depth problem.

The security blindspot. 96% of business leaders acknowledge that generative AI increases the likelihood of a security breach, yet only 24% have taken steps to secure their AI projects. Samsung engineers uploaded proprietary source code to ChatGPT. Employees across every industry paste customer data, financial records, and internal communications into AI tools daily without understanding where that data goes or who can access it. The Stanford AI Index reported that publicly documented AI safety incidents rose 56.4% year over year, from 149 incidents in 2023 to 233 in 2024. These aren't theoretical risks. They are happening now, at scale.

Shadow AI is the new Shadow IT. Remember Chapter 4, where we talked about employees signing up for cloud services without going through IT security review? The same thing is happening with AI tools, but at ten times the speed. When policies are ambiguous, people either default to "no" or, worse, use AI quietly without oversight. Most organizations don't even have a complete inventory of the AI systems operating inside their walls. We've worked with clients who were surprised to learn that their HR screening tool, their customer support chatbot, their fraud detection algorithm, and their email filtering system all qualify as AI systems under emerging regulations. When we ask "do you use AI?" they say no. When we audit their technology stack, we find a dozen AI-powered tools nobody thought to classify that way.

AI systems treated like harmless tools. In 2025, security researchers discovered that McDonald's AI-powered hiring platform was accessible through a test account using the default credentials "123456" with no multi-factor authentication, exposing data linked to 64 million job application records including full chat transcripts with the hiring chatbot. ISACA reviewed the top AI incidents of 2025 and concluded: "The biggest AI failures weren't technical. They were organizational: weak controls, unclear ownership and misplaced trust." Organizations treat AI chatbots like office supplies when they should be governed like powerful engineer accounts with privileged access, rate limits, logging, and monitoring.

Bias hiding in plain sight. A federal judge allowed a nationwide class action lawsuit to proceed against Workday after its AI screening tools allegedly discriminated against applicants based on age, race, and disability, with over 200 qualified candidates disqualified solely based on age. The court ruled that AI vendors can be held liable as "agents" of the employers who use them. A Cedars-Sinai study found that leading AI models generated less effective psychiatric treatment recommendations for African American patients compared to white patients under similar conditions. AI image systems were found to rate Black women wearing natural hairstyles as less intelligent and less professional. These aren't edge cases. They are the predictable outcome of deploying AI systems without governance, bias testing, or human oversight.

The vendor risk chain. If you use third-party AI tools (and almost every company does), you inherit their AI risks. Your chatbot provider's bias becomes your bias. Your AI vendor's training data practices become your liability. For many organizations, the third-party AI risk is actually larger than the internal one. Yet most vendor risk assessment processes were designed for traditional software, not AI-powered tools that learn, adapt, and make autonomous decisions.

Compliance teams built for a pre-AI world. About 40% of enterprises report that they lack adequate AI expertise internally. Your compliance team knows SOC 2 trust services criteria. They know HIPAA safeguards. They know PCI data security standards. But AI governance introduces entirely new concepts: algorithmic bias testing, model transparency documentation, AI impact assessments, training data governance, and human oversight requirements. PwC's 2025 Responsible AI survey found that while 60% of leaders say Responsible AI boosts ROI and efficiency, nearly half said turning those principles into operational processes has been their biggest challenge. The skills gap is real, and it's not closing on its own.

Public trust is declining. Trust in AI companies dropped from 50% to 47% in 2025 as documented incidents multiplied. Deepfake videos impersonating public figures became routine enough to drain savings from seniors who trusted the fabricated endorsements. 64% of organizations cite concerns about AI inaccuracy, 63% worry about compliance issues, and 60% identify cybersecurity vulnerabilities, but far fewer have actually implemented safeguards. The gap between knowing you have a problem and doing something about it is where breaches, lawsuits, and regulatory fines live.

Tools, Resources, and Solutions

ISO/IEC 42001 uses the same Plan-Do-Check-Act methodology as ISO 27001. If you've been through an ISO 27001 certification, the structure will feel familiar. It requires policies, risk assessments, documented controls, internal audits, and management reviews. The certification requires compliance with 38 controls organized into 9 control objectives, and an independent audit by an accredited certification body to earn the designation.

But here's what makes it different from ISO 27001. Information security asks: "Is your data secure?" AI governance asks: "Is your AI trustworthy?" That's a much harder question. Security has right and wrong answers. Trustworthiness involves judgment calls about fairness, explainability, and the impact of automated decisions on real people.

In practice, an AI Management System requires the following.

An AI policy approved by leadership. Not a vague commitment to "responsible AI" on your website, but a documented policy defining how your organization develops, deploys, monitors, and retires AI systems.

An AI inventory. You cannot govern what you haven't mapped. Document every AI system in use across your organization, including third-party tools. Classify each system by risk level. Identify the data it processes, the decisions it influences, and the people it affects. This is where most organizations should start, because the findings are almost always surprising.

An AI risk assessment process for each system you operate. What risks does it pose in terms of bias, accuracy, transparency, privacy, security, and impact on individuals? What is the likelihood and severity of those risks? How are you treating each one?

An AI impact assessment for systems that affect people directly. This is the hard question: "What happens to a real person if this algorithm gets it wrong?" If your AI makes decisions about hiring, lending, healthcare, insurance, or access to services, you need to evaluate the potential impact on the individuals affected.

Controls for data governance, model lifecycle management, transparency, human oversight, and third-party AI management. Many of these overlap with controls you've already implemented for ISO 27001 or SOC 2, which is good news for organizations with existing compliance programs to build on.

Monitoring and continuous improvement. AI systems don't stay static. Models drift. Training data becomes stale.

New risks emerge as capabilities evolve. Your governance framework needs to evolve with them.

The good news for organizations already running ISO 27001: you've done roughly 60 to 70 percent of the work. The management system structure is identical. Risk assessment methodology, internal audit processes, management review cadences, document control, corrective action procedures, all of that transfers directly. The incremental work is the AI-specific layer: bias testing protocols, model transparency documentation, AI risk and impact assessments, and the controls unique to AI governance. Adding ISO 42001 is an expansion of your existing program, not a rebuild from scratch.

The NIST AI Risk Management Framework (AI RMF) is the U.S. counterpart and provides a voluntary, non-certifiable framework organized around four core functions: Govern, Map, Measure, and Manage. It's a solid starting point for organizations that want to build an AI governance program before pursuing formal certification. The AI RMF Playbook offers detailed, practical guidance for implementation.

Microsoft has already achieved ISO 42001 certification for its Copilot products. Cornerstone announced certification in December 2025. Major enterprise buyers are starting to include AI governance in their vendor security questionnaires. We've watched this exact pattern play out with SOC 2 and ISO 27001 over the past decade. Five years ago, having a SOC 2 report was a differentiator. Today, you can't close an enterprise deal without one. AI governance certification is on the same trajectory, just moving faster.

For mid-market companies without a dedicated AI governance team, this is where a trusted advisor makes the difference. The organizations moving fastest on ISO 42001 are the ones that recognized early that AI governance, like cybersecurity itself, is not a DIY project for companies whose core business is building products, serving customers, and growing revenue.

The first-mover advantage is real. The companies that certify now will have the proof their competitors are still scrambling to produce when enterprise customers make AI governance a procurement requirement. And based on every pattern we've seen in cybersecurity compliance over the past two decades, that day is coming sooner than most people think.

What This Means for Your Business

If your company develops, deploys, or uses AI in any form, governance is no longer optional. The EU AI Act enforcement begins August 2026 with fines up to 7% of global revenue. 87% of AI projects fail to reach production, often because they were launched without strategy, governance, or risk assessment. Your enterprise customers will soon require proof of AI governance the same way they require

SOC 2 today. Organizations already certified in ISO 27001 can leverage 60-70% of their existing controls to fast-track ISO 42001 certification. Start with an AI inventory. Map what you have. Classify the risks. Then build governance before the regulators and your customers force you to.

The 90-Day Playbook

Chapter 16: The 90-Day Playbook

> *"Audit-ready in 90 days isn't magic. It's ruthless prioritization."*
> — Author Unknown

The Kitchen Renovation

A friend of mine renovated his kitchen last year. He got three quotes. The first contractor said six months and couldn't give a firm price. The second said four months and kept adding change orders. The third walked in, measured everything, pulled out a binder of previous projects, and said, "Eight weeks. Fixed price. Here's the schedule week by week. I've done 50 of these."

My friend went with the third contractor. Not because he was cheapest. Because he had a system. He'd done it enough times that the unknowns had become knowns. He knew where the pipes would be difficult. He knew which permits would take longest. He knew the exact sequence of demolition, plumbing, electrical, cabinets, and finishing that would eliminate delays. The other contractors were figuring it out as they went. The third one had a playbook.

That's the difference between a 12-month compliance journey and a 90-day one. It's not about cutting corners. It's about having done it enough times that you know exactly what needs to happen, in what order, and where the traps are.

At Careful Security, we've taken over fifty companies from zero to audit-ready using this methodology. SOC 2, ISO 27001, ISO 42001, HIPAA, PCI DSS. The average completion time is 87 days. The first-attempt audit pass rate is 100%. Zero missed deadlines. This chapter walks you through how it works.

Organizational Realities

Before we get into the methodology, let's talk about why compliance takes most organizations 9 to 12 months and why so many attempts fail entirely.

The DIY trap is real. When companies decide to handle compliance internally, the typical pattern looks like this.

Month 1 and 2: the team is confident and making progress. Month 3 and 4: they realize it's harder than expected. Month 5 and 6: panic sets in as the audit date approaches. Month 7: an emergency call to a consultant, except now the work is rushed and more expensive than if they'd started with help. According to industry data, DIY compliance attempts take 12 to 18 months on average, and 60% fail their first audit. That failed audit costs $15,000 or more to remediate, plus the lost months of engineering time that could have been spent building product.

The true cost of DIY is almost always underestimated. Organizations imagine it will take 40 to 50 hours of internal time. The reality is closer to 300 to 500 hours. A senior engineer spending 300 hours on evidence collection at $150 per hour represents $45,000 in opportunity cost. Add a security lead at 150 hours and a project manager coordinating at 50 hours, and the "free" approach costs north of $80,000 in lost productivity, with no guarantee of passing the audit.

Traditional consultants aren't much better. The Big 4 consulting firms (Deloitte, PwC, EY, KPMG) deliver compliance in 9 to 12 months for $100,000 or more, and they staff the engagement with junior consultants. They provide advisory services, meaning they tell you what to do and hand you a binder of recommendations. The actual work, writing policies, implementing controls, collecting evidence, fixing gaps, still falls on your team. That's the fundamental disconnect. Most companies don't have a compliance team. They have an IT team that's already stretched thin trying to keep the lights on.

National boutique firms like Coalfire and A-LIGN are credible alternatives but typically run 4 to 6 months and still operate primarily in advisory mode. The policies require heavy customization. The evidence collection is manual, relying on spreadsheets and email threads. The timeline extends because no one is working on compliance full-time on your side.

Then there's the offshore option. Upwork freelancers and budget consultancies offering SOC 2 for $5,000 to $15,000. The audit failure rate for these engagements runs between 70 and 80 percent. Auditors can spot copy-paste policies immediately. Communication gaps and time zone differences slow progress. And when the audit fails, there's no accountability, no support, and no refund. That $10,000 "savings" becomes a $25,000 loss when you factor in remediation and wasted time.

The pattern across all these approaches is the same: compliance gets treated as a project to be managed rather than a problem to be solved. The deliverable is a binder, not a result. The accountability ends at "we gave you recommendations." And the timeline expands because nobody has done your specific certification enough times to know exactly where the bottlenecks hide.

Tools, Resources, and Solutions

Here's how the 90-day methodology works. We break the engagement into three phases, each with clear milestones and deliverables. The client's team shows up for meetings and provides access. We do the rest.

Phase 1: Build the Foundation. Days 1 through 30.

This is where most of the compliance iceberg lives below the surface. We start with a kickoff workshop, typically two hours with the leadership team, to align on scope, timeline, and responsibilities. Within the first week, we complete the gap analysis: a systematic comparison of the organization's current state against every requirement of the target framework. For SOC 2, that's the Trust Services Criteria. For ISO 27001, it's the Annex A controls. For ISO 42001, it's the 38 AI governance controls across 9 objectives.

The gap analysis tells us exactly what exists and what doesn't. Most mid-market companies already have 30 to 40 percent of the controls in place without realizing it. They're doing access reviews, they have endpoint protection, they run backups. They just haven't documented it in a way that an auditor can verify. The gap analysis separates "things we need to build" from "things we need to document."

Next comes the policy library. We deploy 40 or more customized policies tailored to the organization's size, industry, and technology stack. These aren't generic templates. They're built from a library we've refined across 50+ engagements, then adapted to fit the specific client. This step alone saves 40 to 50 hours compared to writing policies from scratch.

We set up the evidence collection framework in Dashr.ai, our compliance monitoring platform. This is where evidence gets organized, tracked, and made auditor-ready. Instead of spreadsheets and shared drives, every piece of evidence has a control mapping, a collection date, and a status. By the end of Phase 1, the foundation is solid: gaps are identified, policies are deployed, and the evidence engine is running.

Phase 2: Implement Controls. Days 31 through 60.

This is the build phase. Every gap identified in Phase 1 gets closed. Technical controls get implemented: multi-factor authentication across all public-facing systems, endpoint detection and response deployed to every device, logging configured and forwarded to the monitoring platform, access reviews documented, vulnerability scanning scheduled.

Administrative controls get documented: incident response plans, business continuity procedures, vendor risk management frameworks, employee security awareness training. We don't hand the client a template and wish them luck. We write the procedures, configure the tools, and collect the evidence that proves the controls are operating.

This phase includes the risk register, which becomes the organization's living document for tracking and prioritizing security risks. If Chapter 13 (Risky Business) convinced you that risk management shouldn't be a once-a-year exercise, this is where that philosophy becomes operational.

By the midpoint review at day 45, we've typically closed 70 to 80 percent of the identified gaps. The remaining items are usually the ones that require third-party coordination: penetration testing schedules, vendor security questionnaire responses, or tool deployments with longer lead times. We track all of it, and nothing slips through.

Phase 3: Validate and Audit. Days 61 through 90.

This is where the 100% pass rate comes from. Before the real auditor ever sees your environment, we run a mock audit. The mock audit simulates the exact experience: evidence review, control testing, personnel interviews. Every finding gets remediated before the actual audit begins.

We coordinate directly with the auditor, handling scheduling, evidence submission, and questions. The client's team participates in interviews (the auditor needs to hear from the people who operate the controls), but they walk into those interviews prepared because we've briefed them on what to expect and how to articulate what they do.

The audit itself is typically anticlimactic when the preparation is thorough. We've had auditors comment that the evidence was the most organized they'd seen. That's not because our clients are compliance experts. It's because we've done this enough times to know exactly what auditors look for, how they evaluate evidence, and where they probe for weaknesses.

After certification, the engagement doesn't end with a binder on a shelf. Dashr.ai continues monitoring compliance posture in real time: evidence collection, control effectiveness, anomaly detection, and executive dashboards that show security maturity over time. The certification is a point-in-time validation, but the platform ensures you stay compliant between audits. As we discussed in Chapter 14 (The Hammer of Compliance), audits should be more of a spot check and less of a dress rehearsal.

The Framework Overlap Advantage

Here's a practical insight that saves organizations significant time and money. If you need both SOC 2 and ISO 27001, roughly 80% of the controls overlap. That means a combined engagement doesn't cost twice as much or take twice as long. We map the shared controls once and extend coverage to both frameworks. The incremental effort for adding a second framework to an existing engagement is typically 20 to 30 percent, not 100 percent.

The same efficiency applies to ISO 42001. Organizations already certified in ISO 27001 can leverage 60 to 70 percent of their existing management system for AI governance certification. The PDCA structure, the internal audit cadence, the risk assessment methodology, document control, corrective action procedures: all of it transfers directly.

This is where the "ruthless minimalism" philosophy meets compliance strategy. Instead of treating each framework as an independent project, we identify the common controls, implement them once, and map the evidence to multiple frameworks simultaneously. Subtraction beats addition, even in compliance.

What This Means for Your Business

The traditional approach to compliance (12 months, advisory-only, six-figure budget) was built for Fortune 500 companies with dedicated compliance departments. Mid-market companies don't have that luxury. The 90-day methodology exists because your VP of Sales needs SOC 2 to close the enterprise deal this quarter, not next year. Your CFO needs the insurance premium reduction at renewal, not "eventually." Your board needs to see certification before the next funding round, not after. If your team tried DIY and stalled, or if you've been quoted 9 months from a consultant, know that a faster path exists. 50+ companies have taken it. 100% passed their audit. The average completion was 87 days. The question isn't whether 90 days is possible. It's whether you can afford to wait longer.

Acknowledgements

My parents for encouraging me to write a book but stopped asking for updates on the progress. My wife and daughter for allowing unlimited number of coffee shop hours and granting moratorium on the list of daily chores.

Elon Ramirez - without his help this book would never seen the light of the day. I am very grateful to have the opportunity to work with Elon. He personifies what we aspire for. True, sincere and capable. He works with amazing speed and is a man of many talents. He's come up with all the amazing illustrations you see in this book. He's edited, formatted and reviewed this book to make it ready for print.

Our clients – for challenging us constantly to dig deeper and deliver value at every interaction. Without their patronage and latitude we wouldn't have an opportunity to engage in our passion of providing pragmatic cybersecurity services. We learn everyday from their wisdom as we work on resolving their challenges and collaborate on finding solutions.

About the Author

Sammy Basu has worked in cybersecurity for Fortune 100 companies for fifteen-plus years. For the last five years, he has been working as a virtual CISO for clients in the SMB space for a boutique cybersecurity consultancy called Careful Security. Having been exposed to a myriad of issues across different types of organizations, he can easily the commonality in roadblocks faced by organizations championing cybersecurity changes. I have developed perspectives on what works and what doesn't. He holds multiple cybersecurity certifications (CISSP, CISA, SANS GPEN, GMON, and GCCC) and an MS in Information Security.

www.ingramcontent.com/pod-product-compliance
Lightning Source LLC
Chambersburg PA
CBHW052146220526

45471CB00004B/1540